FUNDAMENTALS OF
BECOMING
A BADASS
IN BUSINESS

JOSHUA LEACH-ASLAM

© Copyright 2024 Joshua Leach-Aslam

To my grandfather, Christopher Leach, my hero and mentor, and one of the greatest business minds to walk this planet: Your continuous mentorship has been a beacon, driving me to succeed every step of the way.

And to my wife Sally, and my sons Joshua and Seth: You are the reason I work as hard as I do. I love you with all my heart.

Fundamentals Of Becoming A Badass In Business

Foreword
Why Being Badass is the New Black

Chapter1: The Badass Mindset

Chapter 2: Building Your Empire

Chapter 3: Money Talks, Bullshit Walks

Chapter 4: Influence and Persuasion

Chapter 5: Leadership: Lead Like a Legend

Chapter 6: Innovation and Disruption

Chapter 7: The Ethics of Badassery

Chapter 8: Personal Branding: You Are the Brand

Chapter 9: Building and Leading Badass Teams

Chapter 10: Crisis Management

Chapter 11: Global Domination

Chapter 12: Future-Proofing Your Business

Afterword
keep Being Badass: A Lifelong Commitment

Foreword

Why Being Badass is the New Black

In an era where disruption is the norm and innovation the currency of success, the term 'badass' has transcended its rough-and-tumble origins to embody a new ideal in the business world. Being a badass is about more than just attitude; it's about a distinct, daring approach to life and business that champions the bold over the bland, the remarkable over the routine.

Today's market landscape is more volatile and complex than ever before. With new challenges around every corner, from technological advancements to global competition and market unpredictability, it demands a breed of businessperson that thrives on chaos and transforms it into a ladder to success. This book is for those who see the usual path and choose to forge a new one.

"**Why Being Badass is the New Black**" is more than just a statement, it's an urgent call to arms. Traditional business strategies, while still relevant, are often outpaced by dynamic, unconventional methods. To be badass is to be resilient, decisive, and daring, but also smart, strategic, and ethical. It combines the wisdom of experience with the innovative spirit of the tech age. It's about making waves and never settling for a ripple.

In these pages, you'll discover the transformative power of adopting a badass mindset. This means learning how to confidently make big decisions, influence and inspire those around you, and lead with both courage and consideration. It's about becoming so proficient in the art of business that your very presence commands respect. This book does not just teach you how to survive in the cutthroat world of business, it teaches you how to thrive, dominate, and set the agenda.

A badass doesn't just play the game, they change it for good. They don't just adapt to the market, they set the trends that others follow. And crucially, they understand that their reputation as a leader is built on not just what they achieve but how they achieve it. Badass businesspeople are respected because they combine their ambition with integrity and their tenacity with humility.

So, as we turn the page on traditional business personas and usher in the age of the badass, remember that this isn't about changing who you are. It's about elevating what you're capable of. It's about shedding the conventional in favour of the exceptional. Being badass is the new black because, in today's world, it's the only colour bold enough to represent true business excellence.

Let's embark on this journey together. Let's redefine what it means to be successful in business. Let's be badass.

Chapter 1

The Badass Mindset
Embrace Your Inner Rebel

4

We start this off with a chapter dedicated to the mavericks, the outliers, the game-changers. "Embrace Your Inner Rebel" is more than just a call to arms, it is a manifesto for those ready to challenge the everyday norms and redefine what is possible in the business world. Here, we celebrate those who see the world not just as it is, but as it could be. These are the pioneers who replace the question of "why?" with the audacious "why not?"

Every major innovation in history was once considered an act of rebellion. Breaking through conventional boundaries requires a unique blend of courage, creativity, and a relentless drive to do something different. Consider the career of Howard Schultz, the visionary behind Starbucks' transformation from a local coffee bean store into a global coffee empire. Schultz didn't just set out to sell coffee; he sought to change the concept of the coffee shop as a social experience, fostering a "third place" between home and work where people could relax, meet, or work while enjoying their coffee. This was not about adhering to the existing models of coffee shops; it was about disrupting the entire notion of what a coffee shop could be.

In embracing your inner rebel, you're not discarding every rule and disregarding all wisdom. Instead, it's about discerning which rules to bend and which outdated models to break, all in pursuit of something profoundly better. It's about fostering innovation by thinking differently and being willing to take the risks that others might shy away from.

So, let this chapter serve as your guide to harnessing the power of rebellion for constructive change. Dive into these pages to discover how to cultivate your rebellious spirit responsibly and strategically, to not only innovate but also inspire those around you to embark on the path less travelled.

5

Rebels With a Cause

The first step to embracing your inner rebel is recognising that successful rebellion in business isn't about rebellion for the sake of rebellion. It's directed, purposeful, and grounded in a deep understanding of what you're trying to improve or change. Every disruptive idea that reshaped industries started as a rebellious thought against established norms. Whether it's revolutionising the way people share content online, transforming mundane home appliances into smart devices, or reimagining transportation—these were ideas that initially met resistance. Your inner rebel should be fuelled by a cause—your vision for something better than what currently exists.

Cultivating Courage

Courage is the lifeblood of any rebel. But remember, courage in business isn't about the absence of fear—it's about acknowledging your fears and deciding to move forward anyway. This is easier said than done, of course. It begins with small steps. Start by questioning processes that are done a certain way just because "they've always been done like that." Ask if there's a better, more efficient, or more innovative approach. Then, take your thoughts from questioning to action. Propose new ideas, lead pilot projects, or innovate within your existing role. Each small act of courage builds your confidence and establishes you as a leader who's not afraid to think differently.

Building Resilience

To embrace your inner rebel fully, you must build resilience. The path of a rebel is not an easy one. You will face doubts, not just from others, but from within yourself. You will encounter failures and setbacks. However, resilience allows you to see these as merely steps on the journey. Resilience can be nurtured by maintaining a clear vision and staying connected to your why. Why are you challenging the norm? Why do you believe there is a better way? Keep these questions at the forefront of your mind, and let the answers drive you forward.

Harnessing Your Intuition

Intuition is your inner compass, particularly when navigating uncharted territories. In the business world, data and analytics play critical roles, but some decisions require you to trust your gut. Your inner rebel thrives on intuition because it fills the gaps that logic cannot bridge. To hone this skill, give yourself time for reflection amidst your busy schedule. Reflect on past decisions—what felt right, what didn't, and what outcomes ensued. Strengthening your intuitive sense helps in making swift, confident decisions that often characterise badass leadership.

Staying Educated and Informed

Lastly, a true rebel is always learning. The business landscape is constantly evolving, and staying informed is key to knowing when to make your next move. This doesn't just mean keeping up with your industry news, it means also understanding global events, technological advancements, and emerging market trends. An informed rebel can spot opportunities where others see chaos, and leverage knowledge to drive transformative change.

Embracing your inner rebel is about more than just making noise—it's about making a difference. It's about having the courage to challenge, the resilience to endure, and the wisdom to know when and how to push the boundaries effectively. With this mindset, you are not just participating in the business world; you are actively shaping its future.

Resilience is Key: Thriving in Chaos

In the ever-turbulent seas of business, resilience isn't merely useful, it's essential. This quality separates those who crumble under pressure from those who see chaos as a fertile ground for opportunity. A badass business person not only survives in chaos but thrives, using it as a catalyst for growth and innovation. Here's how you can cultivate and harness resilience to not just withstand the storm, but to steer your ship boldly through it.

Understanding Resilience

Resilience is the ability to bounce back from setbacks, adapt well to change, and keep going in the face of adversity. In the business context, it means maintaining functionality and pursuing goals despite difficulties or delays. It involves a mixture of mental toughness, emotional intelligence, and relentless perseverance. To a badass business leader, resilience means viewing every challenge as an opportunity to learn, adapt, and emerge stronger.

Building a Resilient Mindset

1. **Acceptance**: The first step to building resilience is acceptance. Understand that setbacks are part of the entrepreneurial journey. By accepting that challenges are inevitable, you can shift your focus from feeling victimised by adversity to navigating through it effectively.

2. **Perspective**: Keep challenges in perspective. Instead of magnifying problems, evaluate them as objectively as possible. Ask yourself, "What's the worst that could happen?" Often, you'll find that the fear of the outcome is more paralyzing than the actual setback. Keeping a level head allows you to find solutions more efficiently.

3. **Goals and Action**: Resilient individuals are driven by a clear sense of purpose. They set realistic, actionable goals. When faced with chaos, instead of getting overwhelmed, break down your response into manageable steps and actionable plans. This not only brings clarity but also injects a sense of progress and direction.

Learning from Adversity

Adversity is not a question of "if," but "when." Every challenge you encounter, whether it be a failed project, a missed deadline, or a financial setback, holds within it the seeds of valuable lessons.

These moments of difficulty are not merely obstacles but pivotal opportunities for growth and development.

Embrace Reflection

When adversity strikes, the first step towards transformation is reflection. Take a step back and meticulously analyse the situation. What exactly went wrong? What factors contributed to the setback? More importantly, what actions did you take that were effective, and which ones fell short? This thorough examination is not about assigning blame but about understanding the intricate dynamics at play.

Extracting Insights

Through reflection, extract actionable insights. Identify patterns in your decision-making process that need improvement. Recognise the strengths you exhibited during the crisis—whether it was quick thinking, maintaining calm under pressure, or effective communication. Equally, pinpoint the weaknesses that need bolstering. This balanced evaluation forms the bedrock of wisdom and insight, essential qualities for a resilient leader.

Fostering a Culture of Feedback

Inculcate a culture where feedback is not just encouraged but is an integral part of your organisational ethos. Create safe spaces where team members can share their experiences and perspectives without fear of reprisal. When feedback is normalised, it becomes a powerful tool for collective learning. It enables everyone in the organisation to benefit from the lessons learned from individual and team challenges.

Transforming Mistakes into Learning Opportunities

Shift the narrative around mistakes from being synonymous with failure to being viewed as invaluable learning opportunities. When mistakes are de-stigmatised, it fosters an environment where innovation can thrive. Employees feel empowered to take calculated risks and experiment with new ideas, knowing that even if they fail, their efforts will be a stepping stone to improvement.

Building Organisational Resilience

A resilient organisation is one that continuously evolves by learning from its setbacks. Encourage your team to document and share their experiences and the lessons learned. Implement systems and processes that capture this knowledge, ensuring that it is accessible to everyone. Over time, this collective wisdom becomes a strategic asset, making your organisation more adept at navigating future challenges.

Encouraging Continuous Improvement

Adversity should fuel a relentless pursuit of excellence. Establish mechanisms for continuous improvement where feedback loops are short, and iterative progress is celebrated. Use adversity as a catalyst for innovation, prompting the team to find better solutions and more effective strategies. When every team member adopts this mindset, the entire organisation moves forward with a shared vision of resilience and excellence.

Let me wrap this up for you, adversity is an inevitable part of the business journey, but it is also a powerful teacher. By embracing reflection, fostering a culture of feedback, and viewing mistakes as learning opportunities, you can transform challenges into catalysts for growth. As a leader, your ability to learn from adversity will not only enhance your own wisdom and insight but also build a more resilient, adaptable, and innovative organisation. Remember, it's not the adversity itself that defines you, but how you respond to and learn from it.

Cultivating Emotional Strength

Resilience is as much about emotional intelligence as it is about mental strength. Developing your emotional intelligence involves:

- **Self-awareness**: Recognise your emotional triggers and understand how they affect your decisions.

- **Regulation**: Learn to control your emotions so they don't control you. This means not acting on raw feelings but allowing time for calm reflection.

- **Empathy**: Understanding the emotions of others can help mitigate conflicts and build stronger team relationships, which is crucial in times of crisis.

Staying Connected

Build and maintain a supportive network. Connections can provide practical support, valuable advice, and emotional comfort. Networking isn't just about advancing your career; it's about creating a mutual support system that can prop you up during your lows and cheer for you during your highs.

Practicing Self-Care

Lastly, resilience requires energy. You can't be resilient if you're constantly running on empty. Incorporate regular physical activity, adequate sleep, and healthy eating into your routine. Make time for hobbies and relaxation. Self-care isn't selfish—it's a strategic move for long-term success.

Thriving in chaos demands more than just gritting your teeth and bearing it. It requires developing a resilient mindset that embraces challenges, learns from them, and uses them as stepping stones. A badass business person knows that the real test isn't how you avoid falling but how you rise after you fall. So, embrace chaos, for it is in this turmoil that your true potential as a leader is forged.

Breaking the Rules: When and How to Rebel

Being a badass in the business world often means knowing when to comply with the established norms and when to break them. Rebellion, in the context of business, isn't about being reckless or defiant for the sake of it; it's about intelligent dissent when conventional wisdom no longer holds water, or when innovation demands a new path that hasn't yet been paved by predecessors.

Understanding When to Rebel

1. **When the Rules Stifle Innovation**: If existing rules and processes are stifling creativity and innovation, it might be time to challenge them. Companies that once led the market but failed to innovate have found themselves outpaced by nimble, more creative competitors. If the status quo is keeping your business or team from moving forward, it's a clear signal that change is necessary.

2. **When Ethics Are in Question**: If prevailing practices within your company or industry compromise ethical standards, standing against them is not just an act of rebellion, but a necessity. Building a brand with integrity sometimes requires making tough choices that might go against the grain.

3. **When the Environment Has Changed**: Business is not static, and changes in the market, technology, or customer preferences can render old rules obsolete. Adapting to new realities might require setting aside old guidelines to stay relevant and competitive.

How to Rebel Effectively

Where conformity often reigns supreme, true progress demands a spirit of rebellion. But rebellion for its own sake can be futile; the key lies in rebelling effectively. For seasoned business leaders and those rising through the ranks, strategic rebellion is a powerful tool for driving innovation, challenging outdated norms, and forging new paths to success.

To rebel effectively, you must first be informed. Understanding the rules and the reasons behind them equips you with the knowledge needed to challenge them wisely. This isn't about reckless defiance; it's about making well-considered moves that have the potential to reshape your business landscape. Armed with this knowledge, you can articulate a clear vision that outlines not just what you're against, but what you stand for and hope to achieve.

Building alliances is crucial. Change rarely happens in isolation, and having a coalition behind you lends weight to your cause. Timing your challenge for maximum impact and communicating your intentions clearly and respectfully will further your chances of success. Being prepared to face the consequences of your actions with resilience and a willingness to learn will not only demonstrate your commitment but also strengthen your leadership..

Here's how to ensure that your acts of rebellion are successful and not just acts of futility.

For the Business Leader

Be Informed: As a leader, your credibility hinges on your depth of knowledge. Before challenging any rules, fully understand them. Know why they exist and the purpose they serve. This background knowledge will not only prepare you for potential pushback but also help you formulate a stronger case for why these rules should be changed. Your team looks up to you for guidance, and demonstrating a well-informed stance will earn their respect and support.

Have a Clear Vision: Vision is a cornerstone of effective leadership. Know what you want to achieve through your rebellion. Having a clear, actionable plan that outlines the benefits of breaking the old rules will help others see the wisdom in your bold moves. It's not enough to know what you're against; you must know what you're for. This clarity will inspire confidence and rally your team behind your cause.

Gather Support: As a leader, you understand the power of collective effort. Build alliances. Change rarely happens in isolation. Before you take action, talk to stakeholders, and gather support. Having a coalition behind you can lend weight to your challenge and increase your chances of success. Engage key influencers within your organisation who can champion your vision and help drive the change forward.

Choose the Right Time and Place: Timing is crucial in leadership. Launching your challenge during a crisis, or when the company is already grappling with change, might backfire. Choose a moment when you have the attention and energy of key decision-makers, and when the company can afford to think about change. Assess the organisational climate and leverage opportune moments to introduce your ideas.

Communicate Effectively: Your role as a leader involves clear and persuasive communication. When you do decide to break the rules, communicate your reasons clearly and passionately. Be prepared to face resistance and have your arguments ready. Show respect for the old ways even as you advocate for the new. This shows that your rebellion is not born out of disrespect but out of a desire to improve. Your ability to articulate the vision will be key in swaying opinions and garnering support.

Be Prepared to Face Consequences: Leadership comes with the readiness to face consequences. Understand that not all rebellious actions lead to immediate success. You may face setbacks or even failures. Prepare for them and be willing to take responsibility for any fallout. This responsibility demonstrates leadership and commitment to your ideals. Show resilience and the ability to learn from these experiences, which will strengthen your leadership in the long run.

For Someone Developing in a Business

Be Informed: In your journey towards becoming a business leader, knowledge is your power. Before challenging any rules, fully understand them. Know why they exist and the purpose they serve. This background knowledge will not only prepare you for potential pushback but also help you formulate a stronger case for why these rules should be changed. It shows that you are thoughtful and strategic in your approach.

Have a Clear Vision: As you develop your career, having a clear vision is essential. Know what you want to achieve through your rebellion. Having a clear, actionable plan that outlines the benefits of breaking the old rules will help others see the wisdom in your bold moves. It's not enough to know what you're against; you must know what you're for. This clarity will help you gain the trust and support of your peers and supervisors.

Gather Support: Building a network of allies is critical as you climb the corporate ladder. Build alliances. Change rarely happens in isolation. Before you take action, talk to stakeholders, and gather support. Having a coalition behind you can lend weight to your challenge and increase your chances of success. Identify mentors and colleagues who can provide guidance and amplify your voice within the organisation.

Choose the Right Time and Place: Developing your career involves strategic timing. Launching your challenge during a crisis, or when the company is already grappling with change, might backfire. Choose a moment when you have the attention and energy of key decision-makers, and when the company can afford to think about change. Align your initiatives with the company's broader goals and timing for maximum impact.

Communicate Effectively: Effective communication is a valuable skill to develop. When you do decide to break the rules, communicate your reasons clearly and passionately. Be prepared to face resistance and have your arguments ready. Show respect for the old ways even as you advocate for the new. This shows that your rebellion is not born out of disrespect but out of a desire to improve. Your ability to communicate effectively will enhance your influence and leadership potential.

Be Prepared to Face Consequences: As you grow in your career, resilience is key. Understand that not all rebellious actions lead to immediate success. You may face setbacks or even failures. Prepare for them and be willing to take responsibility for any fallout. This responsibility demonstrates leadership and commitment to your ideals. Learning from these experiences and showing resilience will be crucial in your journey towards becoming a seasoned leader.

By following these strategies, whether you are an established business leader or someone developing in your career, you can rebel effectively, driving meaningful change and innovation within your organisation.

Task 1

Mindset Assessment Tool: Use this tool to assess your current mindset and identify areas for growth towards embracing your inner rebel.

Mindset Assessment Tool: Embrace Your Inner Rebel

Instructions: Answer the following questions honestly to assess your current mindset and identify areas for growth in embracing your inner rebel. Rate each statement on a scale of 1 to 5 based on how strongly you agree or disagree (1 = strongly disagree, 5 = strongly agree).

1. **I am comfortable challenging traditional norms and conventions.**

    1 | 2 | 3 | 4 | 5

2. **I see setbacks and failures as opportunities to learn and grow.**

    1 | 2 | 3 | 4 | 5

3. **I often take calculated risks to pursue new opportunities.**

    1 | 2 | 3 | 4 | 5

4. **I embrace change and adapt quickly to new situations.**

    1 | 2 | 3 | 4 | 5

5. **I trust my instincts and intuition when making decisions.**

    1 | 2 | 3 | 4 | 5

6. **I actively seek out challenges to push myself out of my comfort zone.**

    1 | 2 | 3 | 4 | 5

7. **I believe in my ability to create positive change and impact.**

    1 | 2 | 3 | 4 | 5

8. **I value authenticity and being true to myself in all aspects of life.**

1 | 2 | 3 | 4 | 5

9. **I enjoy exploring unconventional ideas and approaches.**

   1 | 2 | 3 | 4 | 5

10. **I inspire others to think differently and challenge the status quo.**

    1 | 2 | 3 | 4 | 5

Scoring:

- Add up your scores for all 10 questions to determine your overall mindset score.
- A higher score indicates a stronger embrace of your inner rebel mindset.

Interpretation:

- 10-20: Opportunity for Growth - Consider ways to cultivate a more rebellious mindset.
- 21-30: Developing Rebel - You possess some rebel traits, but there's room for further growth.
- 31-40: Rebel in Training - You demonstrate a strong embrace of rebel qualities; continue nurturing this mindset.
- 41-50: True Rebel - Congratulations! You embody the spirit of a true badass rebel.

Use the results of this assessment to reflect on areas where you can further develop your inner rebel mindset and embrace bold, unconventional thinking in your business and life.

Chapter 2

Building Your Empire

Identifying Killer Opportunities

In the dog-eat-dog world of business, opportunity isn't just a knock it's a battle cry. It's about seeing what others overlook, seizing what others hesitate to touch, and transforming it into gold. Welcome to the art of identifying killer opportunities the lifeblood of the badass entrepreneur.

In this chapter, we're tearing down the walls of convention and diving headfirst into the wild jungle of possibility. We'll show you how to develop a radar for spotting opportunities in the most unlikely places and turning them into game-changing ventures.

But beware, this isn't a stroll in the park—it's a high-stakes game of strategy and intuition. We'll teach you to read the signs, follow the breadcrumbs, and pounce when the iron is hot. From market gaps to untapped niches, we'll arm you with the tools to sniff out opportunities like a bloodhound on the hunt.

But spotting an opportunity is only half the battle. We'll also show you how to evaluate its potential, assess the risks, and calculate the rewards. Because in the world of badassery, it's not just about taking chances—it's about taking calculated risks that pay off big time.

So buckle up, fellow badass, because the ride is about to get wild. By the time you're done with this chapter, you'll be seeing opportunities where others see obstacles, and turning dreams into reality with the flick of a wrist.

Get ready to embrace the thrill of the chase, the rush of the hunt, and the glory of victory. Because in the world of badass business, the only limit is your imagination—and we're about to shatter it wide open.

Welcome to the jungle of business.

Understanding the Landscape

Before you can spot a killer opportunity, you need to have a deep understanding of the market landscape. This involves more than just knowing your competitors; it includes understanding customer needs, market trends, technological advancements, and regulatory changes. Here's how you can gain a comprehensive view:

1. **Market Research**: Dive deep into market reports, consumer feedback, and competitor analysis. Look for patterns or gaps that indicate unmet needs or emerging trends.

2. **Stay Updated**: Attend industry conferences, subscribe to relevant publications, and engage with thought leaders on social media. Staying at the forefront of industry news can alert you to changes before they become obvious to everyone else.

3. **Network**: Build relationships within your industry and related fields. Often, opportunities come from connections and insights gained through networking.

Spotting Opportunities

Now that you've got your finger on the pulse of the market, it's time to sharpen your senses and uncover the hidden gems that lie beneath the surface. But spotting opportunities isn't just about luck it's about knowing where to look and what signs to watch out for. Here are some key indicators to keep an eye on: With a solid understanding of the market, you can begin to identify potential opportunities. Look for these signs:

1. **Inefficiencies**: Any process or product that is inefficient presents a chance for improvement. If something frustrates you or your customers, there's likely an opportunity to fix it and create value.

2. **Niche Markets**: Sometimes, the most potent opportunities lie in serving niche markets that larger companies

overlook. These niches often have highly dedicated customer bases willing to pay a premium for specialised products or services.

3. **Regulatory Changes**: New regulations can create opportunities for businesses that can adapt quickly. Whether it's a change in environmental standards or data protection laws, being first to comply can give you a competitive advantage.

4. **Technological Advances**: New technologies can disrupt industries overnight. By staying tech-savvy and open to innovation, you can leverage these technologies to create new business models or improve existing ones.

Assessing Opportunities

So, you've cast your net wide and spotted a slew of potential opportunities, it's time to roll up your sleeves and separate the wheat from the chaff. Because let's face it—not every opportunity is a golden ticket to success. To determine which ones are killer opportunities, consider the following:

1. **Scalability**: Can this opportunity grow? The best opportunities are those that can scale, either by expanding into new markets or by serving more customers over time.

2. **Alignment with Core Competencies**: Does the opportunity align with your business's core competencies and values? Pursuing opportunities that stray too far from what your business does best can dilute your brand and overextend your resources.

3. **Risk Assessment**: Evaluate the risks involved. What are the potential downsides, and how will you mitigate them? Ensure that the potential rewards justify the risks.

4. **Resource Availability**: Consider whether you have the necessary resources to seize the opportunity. This includes finances, personnel, and technology.

Strategically Positioning Yourself

Congratulations! You've identified a killer opportunity and assessed its potential with laser precision. Now comes the thrilling part—positioning yourself to seize that opportunity and ride it all the way to the top. Here's how to set the stage for success:

1. **Develop a Clear USP (Unique Selling Proposition)**: Determine what makes your approach unique. How will you differentiate your product or service from others in the market?

2. **Build Strategic Partnerships**: Form alliances that can help you accelerate market entry or strengthen your market position. Choose partners whose strengths complement your weaknesses.

3. **Execute Quickly**: Speed to market can be a critical advantage. Develop a streamlined process for launching new initiatives so you can capitalise on opportunities before your competitors.

4. **Leverage Branding and Marketing**: Develop strong branding and a robust marketing strategy that communicates the value of your new venture clearly and compellingly.

Risk-Taking: Calculated vs. Reckless

Risk-taking is not just a choice—it's a necessity. But as we navigate the treacherous waters of entrepreneurship, it's crucial to understand the fine line between calculated risks and reckless gambles. In this section, we'll delve into the heart of risk-taking, equipping you with the tools and insights needed to strike the perfect balance and steer your ship towards success.

First and foremost, let's define our terms. Calculated risks are those carefully considered gambles that are backed by thorough analysis, strategic planning, and a clear understanding of the potential rewards and consequences. These are the risks that have been weighed, measured, and deemed worth taking in pursuit of greater goals.

On the other hand, reckless risks are those impulsive leaps into the unknown, driven by emotion, ego, or a misplaced sense of invincibility. These are the risks taken without proper analysis or consideration of the potential fallout, often resulting in costly mistakes and setbacks that could have been avoided.

So how do we distinguish between the two? It all comes down to preparation, foresight, and a healthy dose of humility. Before taking any risk, ask yourself: Have I thoroughly researched the opportunity? Have I considered the potential outcomes, both positive and negative? Am I prepared to mitigate the risks and adapt to unforeseen challenges along the way?

By adopting a mindset of calculated risk-taking, you'll be able to embrace uncertainty with confidence and harness it as a powerful catalyst for growth. But remember, risk-taking is not about blindly charging ahead—it's about making informed decisions, trusting your instincts, and being prepared to pivot when necessary. So as you navigate the risky waters of entrepreneurship, remember to tread carefully, but boldly. Embrace risk as a natural part of the journey, but always strive to keep it in check. With the right balance of courage, caution, and calculated thinking, you'll be well-equipped to chart a course towards success, leaving reckless gambles in your wake.

Understanding Risk-Taking

What constitutes a risk in business. Essentially, any action that has a potential for loss is a risk, but not all risks carry the same weight or potential for negative outcomes. Here's how you can start understanding the nuances of business risks:

1. **Identify the Types of Risks: Risks** can be financial, strategic, operational, or reputational. Knowing the type of risk, you're dealing with can help you develop appropriate strategies to manage it.
2. **Probability and Impact:** Evaluate both the likelihood of the risk occurring and the impact it would have on your business. This evaluation will help you prioritise which risks to address first.

Calculated Risk-Taking

Calculated risks are informed risks. They are the product of thorough analysis and strategic planning. Here's how you can ensure your risk-taking is calculated:

1. **Gather Information**: Collect as much data as possible related to the risk. This includes market data, financial forecasts, and historical outcomes of similar decisions.
2. **Analyse Outcomes**: Use the data to predict potential outcomes. Tools like SWOT analysis (Strengths, Weaknesses, Opportunities, Threats) or risk/benefit analysis can be helpful here.
3. **Plan for Contingencies**: Before taking a risk, plan for various scenarios. Have a clear strategy in place for mitigating potential downsides.
4. **Consult with Experts**: Never hesitate to seek advice from experts or mentors. Their experience can provide valuable insights that improve your risk assessments.

5. **Test Incrementally**: If possible, test the risk on a smaller scale before fully committing. This can provide a low-stakes way to gauge potential outcomes.

Reckless Risk-Taking

Reckless risks are taken without adequate planning or consideration of the consequences. They are often based on gut feelings rather than data, and they lack a safety net. Here are some characteristics of reckless risk-taking:

1. **Lack of Preparation:** Jumping into decisions without proper groundwork or understanding of the potential impacts.
2. **Ignoring Data:** Disregarding data that doesn't support your desired course of action, or not bothering to gather data at all.
3. **No Contingency Plans:** Failing to prepare for potential negative outcomes, which can lead to severe consequences if things don't go as hoped.
4. **High Stakes Without Justification:** Risking significant resources without a clear rationale or a proportionate potential return.

Balancing Risk and Innovation

While it's important to manage risk, it's equally important not to let fear of failure stifle innovation. The key is to find a balance where you can pursue innovative ideas with a safety net in place. This involves:

- **Encouraging a Culture of Smart Risk-Taking:** Foster an environment where team members feel safe to propose and experiment with new ideas, knowing that thoughtful risk-taking is supported.
- **Regularly Reviewing Risk Strategy:** As your business grows and the external environment changes, revisit and

adjust your risk strategies to stay aligned with current realities.
- **Learning from Mistakes:** When risks don't pan out, use them as learning opportunities. Analysing what went wrong and why can provide valuable lessons that refine your approach to risk in the future.

The path to building a business empire is paved with risks, but the art of badass business management lies in distinguishing between calculated and reckless risks. By embracing the former and avoiding the latter, you equip your business to navigate the ups and downs of growth with confidence and strategic acumen.

Strategies for Sustainable Growth

Building a business empire isn't just about rapid expansion; it's about ensuring that growth is sustainable over the long term. Sustainable growth means expanding at a rate that your business can manage without compromising its financial health, brand integrity, or operational capabilities. This section outlines effective strategies that can steer your business towards enduring success.

Ensuring your business's financial health is the foundation of sustainable growth. This involves maintaining a robust cash flow, managing debt wisely, and investing in opportunities that promise steady returns. Regular financial audits and strategic financial planning are crucial. A strong financial base allows your business to weather economic fluctuations and invest in growth opportunities without overextending.

Sustainable growth hinges on leveraging and enhancing your business's core competencies. Identify what your business does best and build on those strengths. This could mean investing in employee training, refining your product or service offerings, or developing proprietary technologies that set you apart from competitors. By focusing on your core strengths, you can ensure that your growth is built on a solid and competitive foundation.

Innovation is a key driver of sustainable growth. Encourage a culture of creativity and continuous improvement within your organisation. This can involve investing in research and development, adopting new technologies, and staying ahead of industry trends. By fostering an innovative mindset, you ensure that your business remains relevant and competitive in a rapidly changing market.

Rapid expansion can strain your resources and infrastructure, leading to operational inefficiencies and a decline in service quality. Scale your operations responsibly by ensuring that your infrastructure, workforce, and supply chain can support growth. This may involve phased expansion plans, strategic partnerships, and incremental increases in production capacity. Responsible scaling helps maintain the quality and integrity of your offerings while meeting growing demand.

Incorporating sustainability practices into your business operations not only benefits the environment but also enhances your brand's reputation and long-term viability. This can include reducing waste, optimising resource use, and implementing eco-friendly practices. Consumers and investors increasingly favour companies that demonstrate a commitment to environmental stewardship, making sustainability a smart business strategy.

Building strong, long-lasting relationships with your customers is vital for sustainable growth. Focus on delivering exceptional value and service to retain existing customers while attracting new ones. Implement customer feedback mechanisms to continually improve your offerings and address customer needs. Loyal customers not only provide steady revenue but also become advocates for your brand, driving organic growth through word-of-mouth.

A strong, cohesive organisational culture is essential for sustaining growth. Foster a culture that aligns with your business values and goals, encourages collaboration, and promotes employee engagement and satisfaction. Happy and motivated employees are more productive, innovative, and committed to your business's success. A positive culture attracts top talent and reduces turnover, providing a stable foundation for growth.

Focusing on Core Strengths

In the quest for business growth, it is essential to identify and leverage your core competencies. Understanding what your business does best and focusing on these areas provides a competitive advantage and leads to more efficient and impactful growth. This section delves into the importance of honing in on your strengths and offers strategies to maximise their potential.

Identifying and leveraging your core competencies starts with a deep understanding of your business's unique capabilities and resources. These core strengths are the foundation upon which your business has built its success. By concentrating your efforts on these areas, you can deliver exceptional value to your customers and differentiate your brand in the marketplace. Whether it's a unique product, a superior service, or a proprietary technology, leveraging these strengths can drive sustainable growth and establish a competitive edge.

Investing in innovation within your niche is crucial for maintaining relevance and staying ahead of competitors. Continuous improvement and innovation ensure that your offerings remain fresh and appealing to your target market. This could involve refining existing products, developing new services, or incorporating the latest technologies. By staying focused on your core areas of expertise, you can more effectively allocate resources towards initiatives that enhance your strengths and create new value for your customers.

For example, consider the case of Nike under the leadership of Phil Knight. Knight identified Nike's core strength in designing high-performance athletic footwear. Instead of diversifying into unrelated products, Nike focused on innovating within its niche. This included developing new technologies like Nike Air, expanding into apparel and equipment closely related to their footwear line, and signing endorsement deals with top athletes to enhance their brand. By leveraging its core competencies and continuously innovating within its niche, Nike maintained its market leadership and achieved sustained growth.

Staying focused on your core strengths also means avoiding the temptation to diversify too broadly. While exploring new markets can be beneficial, straying too far from your primary areas of expertise can dilute your brand and spread resources too thin. A targeted approach ensures that your growth initiatives are aligned with what your business does best, leading to more efficient and effective outcomes.

Moreover, focusing on core strengths facilitates better resource allocation. When you concentrate on your primary areas of expertise, you can channel investments into high-impact projects that drive significant returns. This strategic focus helps in building robust capabilities that are difficult for competitors to replicate, thereby solidifying your market position.

So here it is, focusing on your core strengths is a powerful strategy for achieving sustainable growth. By identifying and leveraging your unique competencies, investing in continuous innovation within your niche, and maintaining a targeted approach, you can build a resilient and competitive business. This strategic focus not only enhances operational efficiency and customer satisfaction but also positions your business for long-term success in an ever-evolving market landscape.

Financial Health Management

Prudent Financial Planning: Maintaining a healthy financial status is crucial for sustainable growth. Effective financial planning involves striking a balance between investing in your business's growth and managing cash flow efficiently. Use financial forecasting to anticipate future expenses, ensuring you have sufficient capital to cover both planned investments and unexpected costs. This approach helps prevent cash flow shortages that can derail your growth plans. Regularly review your financial statements to identify trends and adjust your strategies accordingly. By staying on top of your financial health, you can make informed decisions that support long-term stability and growth.

Diversify Revenue Streams: To mitigate risk and enhance financial stability, diversify your sources of income. Relying on a single product or market can make your business vulnerable to market fluctuations. Develop new products or services that align with your core competencies and explore different markets to broaden your customer base. For example, if you run a software company, consider offering complementary services such as consulting or training. Diversifying your revenue streams not only reduces risk but also opens up new growth opportunities, ensuring your business can withstand economic uncertainties and maintain a steady growth trajectory.

Building a Scalable Business Model

Ensure Scalability: As you plan for growth, it is vital to ensure that your business model and operational processes can scale efficiently. Scalability means having systems in place that allow you to increase capacity without a corresponding rise in costs or resources. Standardise processes and implement robust operational frameworks that can handle increased demand. For instance, if you're in manufacturing, investing in automated production lines can help scale output without proportionally increasing labour costs.

Scalable systems enable you to expand smoothly and maintain profitability as your business grows.

Leverage Technology: Embrace technology solutions that streamline operations and enhance efficiency. Implement automation tools to handle repetitive tasks, freeing up your team to focus on strategic activities. Customer relationship management (CRM) systems can help manage customer interactions more effectively, while data analytics tools provide insights that drive better decision-making. By leveraging technology, you can optimise your operations, reduce costs, and scale your business more effectively. For example, e-commerce platforms can automate order processing and inventory management, allowing you to handle larger volumes with ease.

Cultivating Customer Loyalty

Deliver Exceptional Customer Service: Customer loyalty is essential for long-term growth. Ensure that your customer service is responsive, personal, and consistently high-quality. Train your staff to handle customer inquiries and complaints efficiently, and empower them to go the extra mile to delight customers. Personalise your interactions to make customers feel valued and appreciated. By delivering exceptional customer service, you build trust and loyalty, leading to repeat business and positive word-of-mouth referrals.

Engage with Your Customers: Build strong relationships with your customers through regular communication and engagement strategies. Use social media, email newsletters, and other channels to keep customers informed and engaged. Create feedback loops to listen to their needs and preferences, and adapt your offerings accordingly. Engaging with your customers helps you stay attuned to their evolving needs and fosters a sense of community around your brand. For instance, hosting webinars or Q&A sessions can provide valuable insights and strengthen customer relationships.

Expanding Market Reach

Explore New Markets: To sustain growth, look beyond your current customer base for new market segments that align with your business's core competencies. This could involve geographical expansion, entering new industries, or targeting different demographic groups. Conduct market research to identify opportunities and tailor your marketing strategies to appeal to these new segments. Expanding into new markets diversifies your customer base and reduces dependence on any single market.

Strategic Partnerships and Alliances: Form alliances with other businesses that complement your offerings. Strategic partnerships can help you reach new customers, enter new markets, and share the risks and costs associated with growth initiatives. For example, a tech company might partner with a hardware manufacturer to bundle products and offer integrated solutions. Collaborating with partners can amplify your reach and create synergies that drive mutual growth.

Sustaining a Positive Brand Image

Maintain Ethical Standards: Uphold transparent and ethical business practices to build a strong reputation. Conduct your business with integrity, fairness, and respect for all stakeholders. A reputation for ethical behaviour attracts customers, investors, and employees who share your values. It also fosters trust and loyalty, which are crucial for long-term success. Address any ethical issues promptly and transparently to maintain your brand's integrity.

Focus on Corporate Social Responsibility (CSR): Develop and implement CSR initiatives that reflect your business's values and contribute positively to society. Engage in activities that benefit the community, such as environmental sustainability projects or charitable contributions. CSR initiatives not only enhance your brand image but also encourage a deeper connection with your community. They demonstrate your commitment to making a positive impact, which can differentiate your brand and attract socially conscious consumers.

Fostering a Strong Internal Culture

Invest in Your Team: Your employees are your most valuable asset. Invest in training and development programs that keep them motivated and skilled. Provide opportunities for professional growth and create a positive work environment that fosters collaboration and innovation. Recognise and reward employee achievements to boost morale and retention. A well-trained and motivated team is essential for driving sustainable growth and achieving business objectives.

Promote from Within: Whenever possible, fill higher-level positions with internal candidates. Promoting from within provides career paths for your employees and helps maintain a strong organisational culture as you grow. Internal promotions demonstrate your commitment to employee development and loyalty, which can enhance job satisfaction and performance. This practice also ensures that leaders are familiar with the company's values and operations, leading to smoother transitions and continuity.

Encourage Innovation and Creativity: Foster an environment where employees feel safe to express new ideas and take calculated risks. Encourage a culture of innovation by providing resources and support for creative initiatives. Celebrate successes and learn from failures to continuously improve. An innovative culture drives sustainable growth by enabling your business to adapt to changing market conditions and seize new opportunities.

By implementing these strategies, you can ensure that your business not only grows quickly but also builds a strong foundation for continuous, sustainable expansion. This approach guarantees that your business empire remains robust and resilient, capable of weathering market changes and seizing new opportunities as they arise.

Task 2

Opportunity Identification Canvas: Utilise this template to systematically identify and evaluate killer opportunities for business growth.

Opportunity Identification Canvas

Instructions: Use this canvas to systematically identify and evaluate killer opportunities for business growth. Fill out each section to gain clarity on potential opportunities and assess their viability.

Opportunity Description
Breifly describe the potential opportunity or area for business growth.

Market Analysis:
Target Market: Who are the potential customers or target audience for this opportunity?
Market Size: Estimate the size of the market and potential customer base.
Market Trends: Identify key trends, challenges, and opportunities in the target market.

Competitive Landscape:
Competitors: List major competitors in the market.
Competitive Advantage: What sets your business apart from competitors in this space?

Opportunity Viability:
Revenue Potential: Estimate potential revenue and growth opportunities associated with this opportunity.
Cost Analysis: Assess the costs involved in pursuing this opportunity (e.g., development, marketing, distribution).

Risk Assessment:
Risks: Identify potential risks or challenges associated with pursuing this opportunity.
Risk Mitigation: Develop strategies to mitigate identified risks and challenges.

Resource Requirements:
Skills and Expertise: What skills or expertise are needed to pursue this opportunity?
Resources Needed: Identify resources required (e.g., capital, personnel, technology).

Action Plan:
Key Steps: Outline actionable steps to capitalise on this opportunity.
Timeline: Set a timeline for implementation and achievement of milestones.

Evaluation Criteria:
Success Metrics: Define measurable criteria for evaluating the success of this opportunity.
Go/No-Go Decision: Establish criteria for deciding whether to proceed with or abandon the opportunity.

Chapter 3

Money Talks
Bullshit Walks

Welcome to the chapter where money talks and bullshit walks a no-nonsense crash course in the art of negotiation mastery and profit maximisation. In the cutthroat world of badass business, financial prowess isn't just a luxury, it's a necessity. So buckle up, because we're about to dive headfirst into the heart of the money game, equipping you with the tools and tactics needed to come out on top.

Money is more than just currency it's the lifeblood that fuels the fires of badassery in business. Whether you're sealing a deal, striking a bargain, or making a power move, the ability to wield financial power with finesse is what sets the true badasses apart from the rest. And in this chapter, we're going to show you how to do just that.

But make no mistake this isn't your average finance seminar. We're not here to bore you with spreadsheets and balance sheets. No, we're here to cut through the crap and get straight to the point. We're here to teach you the art of negotiation like a seasoned pro, turning every transaction into a strategic move towards domination.

So get ready to roll up your sleeves and dive into realms financial badassery. From mastering the art of negotiation to maximising your profits and navigating financial challenges with ease, we've got everything you need to make deals that count. So, let's get down to business and start making some serious cash because in business, money talks, and bullshit walks.

Finance Essentials for the Fearless

Financial acumen is non-negotiable. To build and sustain a successful empire, you must master the essentials of finance with confidence and clarity. We will equip you with the foundational knowledge and strategies needed to navigate the financial landscape fearlessly.

Understanding Financial Statements

Understanding financial statements is crucial for any business leader. These documents are more than just numbers on a page, they tell the story of your company's financial health, operational efficiency, and overall stability. At the heart of financial literacy lies the ability to interpret three core statements: the balance sheet, the income statement, and the cash flow statement. Each offers a unique perspective on your business's performance, from assets and liabilities to revenue streams and expenses, and ultimately, how cash is flowing in and out of your organisation.

The balance sheet provides a snapshot of your company's financial position at a specific point in time. It details what your business owns (assets), what it owes (liabilities), and the owner's equity. This statement helps you understand the value of your business and assess its solvency and liquidity. The income statement, or profit and loss statement, is a dynamic view of your company's operations over a period of time. It shows revenue, costs, and expenses, ultimately revealing your net profit or loss. This helps you track your performance, understand your profitability, and identify areas where you can cut costs or increase revenue.

The cash flow statement is perhaps the most critical for day-to-day operations. It tracks the inflows and outflows of cash, showing how well your company generates cash to pay its debt obligations and fund its operating expenses. This statement highlights the actual liquidity of your business, ensuring you have enough cash on hand to meet your immediate and short-term financial commitments. By mastering these financial statements, you gain the ability to make informed decisions, strategize effectively, and steer your business towards sustainable growth and success

Key Financial Metrics

Understanding key financial metrics is crucial for making informed decisions and steering your business towards success. This section breaks down the essential financial indicators that every business leader should master, providing a clear picture of your company's performance and guiding your strategic moves. Let's delve into the metrics that matter and see how they can illuminate your path to profitability and growth.

Profit Margin: The profit margin indicates how much of each pound of revenue translates into profit after accounting for expenses. A higher profit margin signifies better efficiency and profitability.

Return on Investment (ROI): ROI measures the profitability of an investment relative to its cost. It helps assess the efficiency of capital deployment.

Debt-to-Equity Ratio: This ratio shows the proportion of debt used to finance a business's assets relative to shareholders' equity. It reflects the financial leverage of the business.

Financial Planning and Budgeting

Budgeting: Develop a comprehensive budget that forecasts revenue and expenses over a defined period. Budgeting helps you allocate resources effectively and monitor financial performance.

Financial Forecasting: Use historical data and market trends to forecast future financial outcomes. This aids in strategic decision-making and risk management.

Mastering these key financial metrics is not just a routine part of running a business; it's the bedrock of strategic leadership and visionary management. By understanding and leveraging these indicators, you can navigate the complexities of the financial landscape with confidence and precision. This knowledge empowers you to make bold, informed decisions that drive your business forward, ensuring sustainable growth and long-term success. With these metrics in your arsenal, you are not just managing a business—you are leading it to greatness.

Capital Management and Funding

Whether you're seeking to optimise your current capital or exploring new funding avenues, understanding these principles is crucial for maintaining liquidity, fuelling expansion, and achieving long-term success.

Capital Structure: Determine the optimal mix of debt and equity to fund operations and growth. Balance risk and return considerations when choosing sources of capital.

Funding Options: Explore various funding options such as equity financing, debt financing, or alternative financing methods like crowdfunding or venture capital.

Risk Management

In chapter 2 we discussed risk taking here we cover strategies like insurance and hedging, which serve as protective measures to safeguard your business against unforeseen challenges. By mastering risk management techniques, you can ensure your business's financial stability and resilience in the face of uncertainty.

Financial Risk Assessment: Identify and assess financial risks that could impact your business, such as market risk, credit risk, liquidity risk, and operational risk.

Insurance and Hedging: Mitigate financial risks through insurance coverage and hedging strategies. Protect your business from unexpected events that could jeopardise financial stability.

It's crucial to recognise that identifying and assessing financial risks is only the first step. The real power lies in proactively implementing strategies to mitigate these risks and safeguard your business. Market risk, credit risk, liquidity risk, and operational risk can each pose significant threats, but with a robust risk assessment framework, you can anticipate potential issues before they escalate.

Insurance and hedging are vital components of this protective strategy. By securing appropriate insurance coverage, you can shield your business from catastrophic losses due to unforeseen events. Hedging, on the other hand, allows you to manage exposure to market volatility and price fluctuations, ensuring financial stability in turbulent times.

By integrating these risk management practices into your business operations, you not only protect your current assets but also fortify your business's future against uncertainty.

Financial Decision-Making

Financial decision-making stands as the linchpin upon which success hinges. From evaluating investment opportunities to implementing cost-effective measures, each decision carries weight in shaping the trajectory of a company's financial health. So, what should you be doing?

Investment Analysis: Evaluate investment opportunities based on risk, return, and strategic alignment with business objectives.

Cost Control: Implement cost-effective measures to optimise expenses without compromising quality or operational efficiency.

By getting to grips with the principles of investment analysis and cost control, businesses can chart a course towards sustainable growth and profitability. With a keen eye for risk, return, and strategic alignment, coupled with judicious cost management practices, businesses can navigate the intricacies of the financial landscape with confidence and clarity.

Financial Literacy and Continuous Learning

Continuous Improvement: Stay informed about financial trends, regulations, and best practices. Invest in developing your financial literacy through courses, workshops, and networking with financial experts.

By mastering these finance essentials, you will empower yourself to make informed financial decisions, drive profitability, and ensure the financial health and sustainability of your business empire. Remember, in the realm of badass business leadership, understanding how money works isn't just an advantage it's a necessity.

Negotiating Like a Pro

Having laid the groundwork in understanding the intricacies of financial statements and metrics, we now pivot towards honing the art of negotiation, a skill essential for every business leader. Negotiating like a pro requires more than just financial acumen; it demands finesse, strategy, and a deep understanding of human psychology. As we transition from deciphering balance sheets to navigating high-stakes deal-making, we carry with us the foundational knowledge needed to leverage financial insights effectively in negotiation scenarios. Let's delve into the strategies and tactics that will empower you to drive favourable outcomes, forge lucrative partnerships, and propel your business towards greater success.

Never Settle for Less

Negotiation is a cornerstone skill for any badass business leader. Whether you're securing a deal with a client, negotiating terms with suppliers, or discussing terms with investors, the ability to negotiate effectively can make or break your success. In this section, we'll delve into the art of negotiation and share strategies to help you achieve optimal outcomes and never settle for less than what you deserve.

Preparing for Negotiation

Know Your Objectives: Clearly define your goals and desired outcomes before entering a negotiation. Understand what you want to achieve and what you're willing to concede.

Understand Your Counterpart: Research the other party's needs, motivations, and constraints. This will enable you to tailor your approach and propose mutually beneficial solutions.

Establish Your BATNA: BATNA (Best Alternative to a Negotiated Agreement) is your fallback plan if negotiations fail. Having a strong BATNA empowers you to negotiate from a position of strength.

Mastering Negotiation Techniques

Active Listening: Listen more than you speak. Pay attention to verbal and non-verbal cues to understand the other party's perspective and identify areas of agreement and contention.

Build Rapport: Establish a positive relationship with the other party. Building rapport can foster trust and openness, making negotiations smoother and more productive.

Focus on Interests, Not Positions: Instead of fixating on specific demands, focus on underlying interests. Understand what each party truly values and explore creative solutions that satisfy those interests.

Be Assertive, Not Aggressive: Assertiveness is about confidently advocating for your interests while respecting the other party. Avoid aggression, as it can damage relationships and undermine the negotiation process.

Negotiation Strategies

Set High but Realistic Targets: Aim high in your negotiations, but ensure your goals are achievable and backed by sound reasoning. This sets a positive tone and encourages ambitious outcomes.

Use Concessions Strategically: Be selective when offering concessions. Use them to secure concessions in return or to build goodwill without compromising your core objectives.

Create Value: Look for opportunities to expand the pie and create value for both parties. Collaborative negotiations that focus on value creation often lead to more sustainable agreements.

Handling Challenges and Deadlocks

Stay Calm Under Pressure: Negotiations can be intense, but maintaining composure is essential. Take breaks if needed to regroup and refocus.

Addressing Impasses: If negotiations reach a standstill, seek common ground, and explore alternative solutions. Brainstorming or involving neutral third parties can help break deadlocks.

Closing the Deal

Closing the deal is a critical juncture in any negotiation process, where all the discussions, strategies, and concessions come to fruition. It's the moment where verbal agreements must be meticulously translated into written commitments to ensure clarity and prevent misunderstandings. Its essential for long-term success to ensure that all parties leave the table satisfied and with a clear understanding.

Summarise and Confirm Agreements: Clearly summarise key points and confirm agreements in writing to avoid misunderstandings.

Maintain Relationships Post-Negotiation: Foster positive relationships even after negotiations conclude. Continued collaboration and goodwill can pave the way for future opportunities.

Successfully closing a deal is more than just a signed contract, it's about cementing a foundation of trust and mutual respect. By clearly summarising key points and confirming agreements in writing, you safeguard your interests and lay the groundwork for smooth implementation. Equally important is the maintenance of relationships post-negotiation. Fostering a positive rapport with your counterparts ensures that any future negotiations start from a place of goodwill and cooperation. As you refine your skills in closing deals, remember that each successful negotiation not only advances your immediate objectives but also strengthens the relational ties that are essential for sustained business success.

Continuous Improvement

Reflect and Learn: After each negotiation, reflect on what went well and what could be improved. Incorporate lessons learned into future negotiations to refine your skills.

By mastering the art of negotiation and adopting a strategic approach, you position yourself to achieve optimal outcomes and never settle for less than what your business deserves. Negotiating like a pro isn't just about getting the best deal, it's about building mutually beneficial relationships and driving long-term success for your business empire.

Profit with a Punch: Maximising Your Margins

In the world of badass business leadership, profitability is not merely about generating revenue, it's about squeezing the most value out of every opportunity and ensuring your margins are maximised. This section delves into the strategic art of enhancing your financial performance with both impact and ingenuity. We will explore a series of powerful, actionable tips designed to boost profitability, streamline operations, and amplify your business's bottom line. As we draw this chapter to a close, these quick tips will arm you with the knowledge and tactics needed to drive your business empire to new heights of financial success. Let's unlock the full potential of your profit margins and make every penny count.

Optimising Pricing Strategies

Value-Based Pricing: Align pricing with the value your product or service delivers to customers. Focus on communicating and emphasising the unique benefits and advantages of your offerings.

Dynamic Pricing: Implement dynamic pricing strategies that respond to market demand and customer behaviour. Use data analytics to adjust prices in real-time for optimal revenue generation.

Streamlining Operations

Identify Cost Drivers: Analyse your cost structure to identify and address key cost drivers. Streamline operations, optimise supply chains, and eliminate inefficiencies to reduce overheads.

Implement Lean Practices: Embrace lean principles to minimise waste and improve productivity. Lean practices enable you to do more with less, enhancing profitability without compromising quality.

Negotiating Supplier Contracts

Negotiate Better Terms: Use your negotiation skills to secure favourable terms with suppliers. Explore bulk discounts, extended payment terms, and strategic partnerships to lower procurement costs.

Enhancing Sales and Marketing Efficiency

Targeted Marketing: Focus marketing efforts on high-value customer segments to maximise returns on investment. Leverage data analytics and customer insights to tailor campaigns for maximum impact.

Upselling and Cross-Selling: Encourage upselling and cross-selling to increase the average transaction value. Offer complementary products or services that add value to customers' purchases.

Customer Retention and Loyalty

Build Strong Relationships: Invest in customer retention strategies to cultivate loyalty and reduce customer churn. Loyal customers are more likely to make repeat purchases and recommend your business to others.

Harnessing Technology for Profitability

Automation: Leverage automation tools to streamline repetitive tasks and reduce labour costs. Automation enhances efficiency and frees up resources for strategic initiatives.

Data Analytics: Harness the power of data analytics to gain insights into customer behaviour, market trends, and operational performance. Use data-driven decision-making to optimise business processes and drive profitability.

Continuous Improvement and Innovation

Continuous Cost Monitoring: Regularly monitor and evaluate costs to identify opportunities for further optimisation. Challenge existing assumptions and explore innovative ways to reduce expenses.

Encourage Innovation: Foster a culture of innovation within your organisation. Encourage employees to propose and implement creative ideas that enhance profitability and drive growth.

Financial Discipline and Strategic Investments

Maintain Financial Discipline: Practice prudent financial management by adhering to budgets, controlling expenses, and monitoring cash flow. Avoid unnecessary expenditures that don't contribute to profitability.

Strategic Investments: Allocate resources strategically to initiatives that offer the highest return on investment. Prioritise projects that align with your business goals and have the potential to generate substantial returns.

Measuring and Monitoring Performance

Key Performance Indicators (KPIs): Define and track relevant KPIs to assess financial performance and profitability. Use KPIs to measure progress towards goals and identify areas for improvement.

You can maximise your margins and drive sustainable profitability for your business empire. Profitability isn't just a financial metric, it's a reflection of your business's ability to create value, adapt to changing market conditions, and thrive in the competitive landscape. With a punchy approach to profitability, you can elevate your business to new heights of success and establish yourself as a true badass in business leadership.

As we wrap up Chapter Three, it's clear that mastering the financial aspects of your business is a cornerstone of achieving true badass status in the business world. From understanding the intricacies of financial statements to negotiating deals like a pro, and from strategic financial decision-making to maximising your profit margins, you've now got a toolkit brimming with powerful strategies to elevate your business acumen.

Throughout this chapter, we've emphasised the importance of financial literacy. We've demystified the complex world of financial statements, helping you to read between the lines and understand the story behind the numbers. This foundation is essential, not just for keeping your business afloat, but for driving it towards sustainable growth and long-term success.

We've also delved into the art of negotiation, where your financial savvy meets strategic communication. Effective negotiation is about more than just striking a deal; it's about forging partnerships that are beneficial in the long run. With these skills, you can navigate high-stakes discussions with confidence, ensuring that every agreement propels your business forward.

Finally, our deep dive into maximising profit margins highlighted the importance of strategic thinking and operational efficiency. By focusing on boosting profitability, you can ensure that your business not only grows but thrives in a competitive market. The quick tips provided are designed to be actionable, empowering you to make impactful changes immediately.

Now, armed with this knowledge, you're ready to pounce on opportunities with the prowess of a seasoned entrepreneur. Embrace these financial strategies with the boldness and determination that defines badass business leadership. Your journey towards financial mastery doesn't end here, it's just beginning. As you continue to refine these skills and apply them to your business, remember that every decision, every negotiation, and every profit margin improvement brings you one step closer to building an unstoppable empire.

> **Task 3**
>
> **Negotiation Playbook Template**: Develop your negotiation strategies with this playbook template, including key tactics and approaches.
>
> **Negotiation Playbook Template**
>
> **Instructions:** Use this playbook template to develop effective negotiation strategies for business deals and transactions. Customise each section based on your specific negotiation objectives and circumstances.

1. **Negotiation Objectives:**
- Define your primary objectives for the negotiation (e.g., pricing, terms, timeline).

_____
_____
_____

2. **Preparation:**

- Gather Information: Conduct research on the other party, their needs, and potential alternatives.
- Identify Key Points: Determine your non-negotiables and areas open for compromise.
- Set Goals: Establish target outcomes and fallback positions for each objective.

_____
_____
_____

3. **Negotiation Team:**

- Roles and Responsibilities: Assign roles to team members (e.g., lead negotiator, subject matter expert, note-taker).
- Communication Plan: Define how information will be shared and decisions communicated during negotiations.

_____
_____
_____

4. **Key Tactics and Approaches:**

- BATNA (Best Alternative to a Negotiated Agreement): Identify your BATNA and leverage it during negotiations.
- Anchoring: Set the tone and direction of the negotiation by making the first offer.
- Concessions: Plan strategic concessions to trade off during the negotiation process.

- Active Listening: Listen actively to the other party's concerns and interests to identify mutual gains.

_____
_____
_____

5. **Communication Strategy:**

- Tone and Language: Define the tone and language to use during negotiations (e.g., assertive yet respectful).

- Body Language: Consider non-verbal cues and gestures to convey confidence and understanding.

_____
_____
_____

6. **Counterarguments and Responses:**

- Anticipate Objections: Identify potential objections or pushback from the other party and prepare responses.

- Reframe Issues: Use reframing techniques to shift the conversation towards mutually beneficial outcomes.

_____
_____
_____

7. **Closing Strategies:**

- Trial Closes: Test potential agreements and commitments throughout the negotiation.

- Final Offer: Determine your final offer or counteroffer based on negotiation progress.

_____
_____
_____

8. **Follow-Up and Documentation:**

- Follow-Up Plan: Outline post-negotiation actions, including next steps and timelines.

- Documentation: Record key points, agreements, and action items from the negotiation for future reference.

_____
_____
_____

Use this Negotiation Playbook Template to prepare and execute successful negotiations that drive positive outcomes for your business. Tailor the playbook to suit your negotiation style and adapt strategies based on real-time feedback and insights gained during the negotiation process.

Chapter 4

Influence & Persuasion

In this chapter, we jump into the power dynamics of badass business, exploring the subtle nuances of persuasion, networking grit, and brand persona building. Here, influence isn't just a skill; it's a weapon wielded by the bold, the cunning, and the unstoppable.

In the spirit of decoding the secrets of influence, we draw inspiration from the legendary Warren Buffett, whose masterful use of persuasion and strategic networking has propelled him to the forefront of the investment world. Buffett's ability to communicate his vision, build enduring relationships, and navigate complex negotiations exemplifies the transformative impact of wielding influence with finesse.

Prepare to be captivated as we unravel the mysteries of influence, dissecting its inner workings and unveiling its secrets. From the boardroom to the networking event, from the digital realm to the heart of personal branding, we'll navigate the intricate webs of influence with precision and finesse. Whether you're a seasoned entrepreneur or a budding business mogul, mastering the art of influence and persuasion is essential for carving out your place in the cutthroat world of business.

So, buckle up, because we're about to embark on a journey into the heart of influence and persuasion, a journey that will challenge your perceptions, expand your horizons, and equip you with the tools needed to wield influence like a true badass. Get ready to unleash your inner persuader, forge powerful connections, and build a brand persona that commands attention. The stage is set, the players are ready, let the games begin.

The Art of Persuasion: Winning Minds and Hearts

In leadership, the ability to influence and persuade others is a critical skill. Whether you're rallying your team around a vision, convincing investors to fund your venture, or securing buy-in from stakeholders, mastering the art of persuasion can elevate your leadership impact. This chapter explores effective strategies for winning minds and hearts, leveraging influence ethically and strategically.

At the core of persuasion is the ability to communicate a compelling vision that resonates with your audience. It's not just about presenting facts and figures; it's about storytelling, crafting narratives that connect on an emotional level and inspire action. To persuade effectively, you must understand the needs, desires, and motivations of your audience. This empathy allows you to tailor your message in a way that speaks directly to their interests and concerns, making your vision not just understandable but irresistible.

Building credibility is another pillar of effective persuasion. People are more likely to be influenced by those they trust and respect. This means demonstrating expertise, maintaining integrity, and consistently delivering on promises. By establishing yourself as a credible leader, you create a foundation of trust that makes it easier to sway opinions and gain support. Remember, persuasion is not about manipulation; it's about fostering genuine belief in your ideas through honest and transparent communication.

Active listening plays a crucial role in persuasion. Engaging in two-way communication, where you listen as much as you speak, helps to build rapport and understanding. By actively listening to the concerns and feedback of others, you show that you value their input, which in turn makes them more receptive to your ideas. This collaborative approach not only strengthens relationships but also enhances your ability to refine your message and strategy based on the insights you gather.

Leveraging social proof is another powerful persuasion strategy. People tend to follow the actions of others, especially when they are uncertain. Highlighting testimonials, case studies, or endorsements from respected figures can significantly boost your persuasive efforts. By showing that others support your vision or have benefited from your ideas, you reduce perceived risk and increase the likelihood of buy-in.

As we delve deeper into this chapter, we'll explore the nuances of ethical persuasion. It's essential to use your influence responsibly, ensuring that your persuasive tactics align with your core values and the best interests of your audience. Persuasion should foster trust, promote collaboration, and drive positive outcomes, not manipulate or coerce.

Looking ahead, we will transition from the theoretical aspects of persuasion to practical applications. You'll learn specific techniques and approaches for various scenarios, from team leadership to investor pitches and stakeholder management. These insights will empower you to harness the full potential of your persuasive abilities, making you a more effective and influential leader.

Understanding the Power of Persuasion

Ethical Influence vs. Manipulation: Differentiate between ethical influence, which seeks to persuade through honesty and integrity, and manipulation, which employs deceptive or coercive tactics. Aim to influence ethically, respecting the autonomy and interests of others.

Building Credibility and Trust: Establish credibility by demonstrating competence, integrity, and reliability. Earn trust through transparency, consistency, and genuine concern for others' well-being.

Effective Persuasion Techniques

Appeal to Emotions: Emotions play a significant role in decision-making. Use storytelling, empathy, and emotional appeals to connect with your audience on a deeper level.

Highlight Benefits and Value: Clearly articulate the benefits and value of your ideas or proposals. Explain how they address specific needs or solve problems for your audience.

Use Social Proof: Leverage social proof by showcasing testimonials, case studies, or success stories that demonstrate the positive outcomes of adopting your ideas.

Reciprocity: Offer value upfront to trigger a sense of obligation or reciprocity in your audience. This could be in the form of valuable insights, resources, or favours.

Building Rapport and Connection

Active Listening: Demonstrate genuine interest by actively listening to others' perspectives and concerns. Validate their feelings and show empathy.

Mirror and Match: Subtly mirror the body language, tone, and pacing of your audience to build rapport and create a sense of familiarity.

Influencing Organisational Dynamics

Navigating Hierarchies: Understand the power dynamics within your organisation and adapt your approach accordingly. Build alliances with key stakeholders and influencers.

Strategic Alliances: Form strategic partnerships and alliances to amplify your influence and broaden your reach. Collaborate with influential individuals or groups who share your vision.

Overcoming Resistance

Addressing Objections: Anticipate and address potential objections or concerns upfront. Be prepared to provide evidence, data, or alternative solutions to alleviate doubts.

Handling Conflict: Manage conflict constructively by focusing on common goals and interests. Seek win-win solutions that satisfy all parties involved.

Adapting Communication Styles

Tailor Your Message: Customise your message to resonate with different audiences. Adapt your communication style based on the preferences and priorities of your listeners.

Continuous Improvement

Seek Feedback: Solicit feedback from trusted peers or mentors to refine your persuasion skills. Learn from both successes and failures to continually enhance your approach.

Practice Empathy and Authenticity: Cultivate empathy and authenticity in your interactions. Genuine concern for others' perspectives and well-being strengthens your influence and fosters lasting relationships.

Through the art of persuasion and ethical influence, you can inspire action, drive change, and achieve remarkable results in your business endeavours. Winning minds and hearts isn't just about getting your way, it's about forging meaningful connections, building consensus, and leading with impact. Influence, when wielded responsibly, is a powerful tool for shaping the future and leaving a lasting legacy as a badass business leader.

Playing the Game: Networking with Grit

Networking is a cornerstone of business leadership, acting as the lifeblood of your professional growth and organisational success. It's through these valuable connections that you gain access to insights, resources, and opportunities that can propel your business empire forward. However, effective networking requires more than just attending events and exchanging business cards; it demands grit, approaching relationships with determination, authenticity, and strategic intent.

Determination in Networking

Networking with determination means actively seeking out opportunities to connect with others, even when it feels challenging or outside your comfort zone. This involves setting clear networking goals, such as meeting a certain number of new contacts per month or targeting specific industry events. Determination also means following up persistently, ensuring that initial connections turn into meaningful relationships. By approaching networking with a relentless drive, you position yourself to uncover opportunities that might otherwise remain hidden.

Authenticity in Relationships

Authenticity is the bedrock of meaningful networking, and it's what differentiates superficial contacts from truly impactful connections. Building genuine relationships requires a commitment to honesty, openness, and a sincere interest in others. When you approach networking with authenticity, you're not just exchanging business cards; you're creating a foundation for lasting, mutually beneficial relationships.

Rather than focusing solely on what you can gain from a connection, shift your mindset to consider how you can add value to the other person. This could be through sharing valuable insights, offering support, or connecting them with someone in your network who can help them achieve their goals. This reciprocity fosters trust and respect, which are essential for long-term collaboration and partnership. When people see that you are genuinely invested in their success, they are more likely to reciprocate with the same level of commitment.

Sharing your experiences candidly helps to establish a deeper connection. Be willing to discuss both your triumphs and your challenges, as this vulnerability can create a stronger bond. People appreciate transparency and are more likely to open up about their own experiences when they see you doing the same. Active listening is crucial in this process. Pay attention to what others are saying, ask thoughtful questions, and show empathy towards their challenges and successes. This demonstrates that you value their perspective and are engaged in the conversation.

Empathy goes hand-in-hand with authenticity. By understanding and acknowledging the emotions and experiences of others, you build a connection based on mutual respect and understanding. Show genuine concern for their well-being and celebrate their successes as if they were your own. This emotional intelligence can significantly enhance the quality of your interactions and lead to deeper, more meaningful relationships.

Authentic relationships are more likely to withstand the test of time and provide mutual benefits. They are built on a foundation of trust and mutual respect, making them resilient in the face of challenges and changes. Such relationships can lead to long-term collaborations, partnerships, and opportunities that might not have been possible through more superficial connections.

Moreover, authenticity in networking can have a ripple effect, influencing the broader culture of your professional community.

When you lead with authenticity, you inspire others to do the same, creating an environment where genuine connections and mutual support are the norms. This can foster a more collaborative and innovative community, benefiting everyone involved.

Strategic Intent in Building Your Network

Strategic intent involves being purposeful about who you connect with and why. Identify key individuals and organisations that align with your business goals and values. This might include potential mentors, industry leaders, or partners who can provide unique insights and opportunities. By strategically expanding your network, you ensure that each connection has the potential to contribute significantly to your professional journey. Use tools like LinkedIn to research and connect with individuals who can help you achieve your strategic objectives.

Maximising Networking Opportunities

Networking opportunities are abundant, but maximising their potential requires preparation and engagement. Attend industry conferences, seminars, and workshops where you can meet like-minded professionals. Prepare an elevator pitch that succinctly communicates your value proposition and goals. During events, engage in meaningful conversations rather than surface-level chit-chat. Ask insightful questions and show genuine curiosity about others' work. After the event, follow up with personalised messages to reinforce the connection and explore ways to collaborate.

Leveraging Digital Platforms

In today's digital age, networking extends beyond face-to-face interactions. Utilise digital platforms like LinkedIn, Twitter, and industry-specific forums to connect with professionals globally. Join relevant groups and participate in discussions to increase your visibility and credibility. Share valuable content and insights that showcase your expertise and engage with others' posts to build rapport. Digital networking allows you to maintain and grow your network regardless of geographical constraints.

Creating a Supportive Network Ecosystem

A powerful network is not just about individual connections but also about creating an ecosystem of support. Foster a community where members of your network can connect with each other, share resources, and collaborate. Act as a connector, introducing people who can benefit from each other's expertise and experience. This not only strengthens your network but also positions you as a valuable hub within your professional community.

Measuring Networking Success

Finally, measure the success of your networking efforts by evaluating the quality and impact of your connections. Reflect on how your network has contributed to your personal and professional growth. Are you gaining valuable insights, opportunities, and support? Are your connections resulting in collaborations and business growth? Use these metrics to refine your networking strategy and ensure it continues to align with your goals.

Networking with grit is about combining determination, authenticity, and strategic intent to build a powerful and supportive network. By approaching networking with purpose and passion, you can forge relationships that not only propel your business forward but also enrich your professional journey.

Social Media Savvy: Building Your Brand Persona

In today's digital age, establishing a strong presence on social media is essential for cultivating your brand persona and expanding your influence as a badass business leader. Social media is more than just a platform for promotion; it's a powerful tool for storytelling, engagement, and building meaningful connections with your audience. This section delivers those quick fire strategies for leveraging social media platforms to build your brand persona authentically and strategically, ensuring that your online presence reflects your values, vision, and expertise.

To begin with, authenticity is key. In a world where audiences are bombarded with content, being genuine sets you apart. Share your journey, the highs and the lows, so that your audience can see the real person behind the brand. This transparency builds trust and loyalty, making followers more likely to engage with and support you. Remember, people connect with people, not just logos or corporate messages. Showcasing your personality, values, and behind-the-scenes moments can humanize your brand and create a deeper connection with your audience.

Consistency across platforms is another critical element of building your brand persona. Whether you're on LinkedIn, Twitter, Instagram, or Facebook, your messaging, tone, and visual style should be cohesive. This consistency reinforces your brand identity and makes it easier for your audience to recognise and remember you. Develop a content strategy that outlines your key themes, posting frequency, and engagement tactics. This strategy will help you maintain a steady and coherent presence across all your social media channels.

Engagement is the crux of social media. It's not enough to just post content; you must actively engage with your audience. Respond to comments, participate in discussions, and show appreciation for your followers' support. Engaging with your audience in a meaningful way fosters a sense of community and makes your followers feel valued. Use polls, Q&A sessions, and live videos to interact with your audience in real-time, creating opportunities for deeper engagement and connection.

Leveraging analytics is crucial for refining your social media strategy. Social media platforms provide a wealth of data about your audience's behaviour and preferences. Pay attention to metrics like engagement rates, reach, and follower growth to understand what content resonates most with your audience. Use these insights to tailor your content and posting schedule, ensuring that you're meeting the needs and interests of your followers.

Collaborations and partnerships can also amplify your social media presence. Partner with influencers, thought leaders, and brands that align with your values and vision. These collaborations can introduce you to new audiences and add credibility to your brand. Co-hosting webinars, live sessions, or creating joint content can be a powerful way to expand your reach and influence.

Finally, staying updated with social media trends and platform features is essential for maintaining a competitive edge. Social media is constantly evolving, with new features and trends emerging regularly. Stay informed about these changes and be willing to experiment with new formats and strategies. Whether it's embracing the latest trend on TikTok or using LinkedIn's new features for professional networking, staying adaptable will help you keep your content fresh and engaging.

Building your brand persona on social media is a multifaceted process that requires authenticity, consistency, engagement, analytics, and adaptability. By leveraging these strategies, you can create a powerful and influential social media presence that not only enhances your brand but also builds a loyal and engaged community around it.

Top 15 Tips for Building Your Brand Persona on Social Media

If your still umming and arh'ing, lets wrap this up as a top tip section, simplicity is the essence of this book.

1. **Define Your Brand Voice**:

Establish a clear and consistent brand voice that reflects your values and personality. Whether it's professional, casual, humorous, or inspirational, your voice should be recognisable across all platforms.

2. **Know Your Audience**:

Conduct thorough research to understand who your audience is, what they care about, and how they interact on social media. Tailor your content to meet their interests and needs.

3. **Create High-Quality Content**:

Invest in creating high-quality visuals, videos, and written content. Use professional photography, graphic design tools, and engaging copy to capture attention and convey your message effectively.

4. **Be Consistent**:

Consistency is key in building a recognisable brand. Maintain a regular posting schedule and ensure your visual and written content aligns with your brand identity.

5. **Engage with Your Audience**:

Don't just post and forget. Engage with your audience by responding to comments, answering questions, and acknowledging feedback. This interaction builds a loyal community.

6. **Use Stories and Live Features**:

Utilise features like Instagram Stories, Facebook Live, and LinkedIn Live to share real-time updates and engage with your audience. These formats are great for behind-the-scenes content and spontaneous interactions.

7. **Leverage User-Generated Content**:

Encourage your followers to create content related to your brand. Reposting user-generated content not only provides social proof but also fosters a sense of community and engagement.

8. **Run Contests and Giveaways**:

Organise contests and giveaways to boost engagement and attract new followers. Make sure the prizes are relevant to your brand and appealing to your target audience.

9. **Collaborate with Influencers**:

Partner with influencers who align with your brand values and have a strong following within your target market. Influencers can help amplify your message and reach new audiences.

10. **Analyse Your Performance**:

Regularly review your social media analytics to understand what works and what doesn't. Adjust your strategy based on data-driven insights to improve engagement and reach.

11. **Tell Your Story**:

Use your social media platforms to tell your brand's story. Share your journey, mission, values, and the people behind the brand. Storytelling creates an emotional connection with your audience.

12. **Utilise Hashtags Effectively**:

Research and use relevant hashtags to increase the discoverability of your content. Create a branded hashtag for your business to encourage community engagement and track user-generated content.

13. **Stay Updated with Trends**:

Keep an eye on social media trends and adapt your strategy accordingly. Participate in popular challenges, use trending hashtags, and stay relevant to keep your audience engaged.

14. **Invest in Paid Advertising**:

Consider using paid social media advertising to boost your reach and target specific demographics. Platforms like Facebook,

Instagram, and LinkedIn offer advanced targeting options to ensure your ads reach the right audience.

15. **Showcase Testimonials and Reviews**:

Highlight positive testimonials and reviews from customers to build credibility and trust. Share these on your social media channels to demonstrate the value and quality of your products or services.

By building a compelling brand persona on social media, you can strengthen your influence, attract new opportunities, and foster meaningful relationships with your audience. Social media isn't just a promotional tool it's a powerful platform for expressing your brand's identity, values, and vision, establishing yourself as a respected authority in your industry, and making a lasting impact as a badass business leader.

As we draw the curtains on this chapter, it's time to reflect on the journey we've embarked upon the exhilarating exploration of influence and manipulation in the world of badass business. From mastering the art of persuasion to navigating the intricate webs of networking and building a brand persona that commands attention, we've delved deep into the realm of influence, equipping you with the tools and insights needed to wield it with finesse.

But influence is more than just a tool—it's a double-edged sword that must be wielded with care and responsibility. As we've learned, the power of persuasion can be a force for good, inspiring action, driving change, and propelling businesses towards success. But it can also be a weapon, used to manipulate, deceive, and exploit for personal gain.

So as you navigate the murky waters of influence in the world of badass business, remember to wield your power wisely. Use it to uplift, empower, and inspire those around you, and never lose sight of the values that define you as a leader. With the right mindset, integrity, and a commitment to ethical conduct, you'll not only influence minds but also shape hearts, leaving a lasting legacy of impact and inspiration in your wake.

As we bid farewell to this chapter, let us carry forward the lessons learned and the insights gained, ready to wield the power of influence with wisdom, grace, and unwavering badassery. For in the world of business, influence is the currency of success, and with it, anything is possible.

Task 4 is about creating a Networking Action Plan, Use the Template to take intentional steps towards expanding your professional network, building relationships, and leveraging opportunities for career growth and development.

Task 4

Create a personalised action plan for effective networking with grit using this template.

Networking Action Plan Template

Instructions: Use this template to create a personalised action plan for effective networking with grit. Develop specific goals and strategies to expand your professional network and build meaningful connections.

Networking Goals:

- Define your objectives for networking (e.g., expanding industry connections, building partnerships, seeking mentorship).

Target Audience:

- Identify specific individuals or groups you want to connect with (e.g., industry influencers, potential collaborators, experts in your field).

Networking Strategy:

- Events and Activities: List networking events, conferences, or workshops to attend.
- Online Platforms: Identify social media platforms or professional networks for connecting virtually.
- Networking Groups: Join industry-specific groups or associations to expand your network.

Personal Branding:

- Elevator Pitch: Craft a concise introduction that highlights your skills, expertise, and unique value proposition.
- LinkedIn Profile: Update your LinkedIn profile to reflect your professional brand and interests.

Outreach Plan:

- Cold Outreach: Develop a strategy for reaching out to new contacts via email or LinkedIn messages.
- Warm Introductions: Leverage existing connections for warm introductions to key individuals.

Follow-Up Strategy:

- Schedule Follow-Ups: Set reminders for following up with new contacts after initial interactions.

- Value Exchange: Offer value (e.g., sharing industry insights, resources) to strengthen relationships.

Networking Metrics:

- Connection Targets: Set monthly or quarterly targets for expanding your network.
- Engagement Metrics: Track interactions (e.g., meetings, emails) to evaluate networking effectiveness.

Continuous Improvement:

- Reflection: Reflect on networking experiences and adjust strategies based on feedback and outcomes.
- Learning Opportunities: Seek feedback from mentors or peers to refine networking skills.

Chapter 5

Leadership
Lead Like a Legend

Welcome to the inner sanctum of badassery, where success isn't just measured by individual accomplishments but by the collective power of a badass team. We're about to embark on a journey into the heart of leadership, where the true magic happens: building teams that defy the odds, challenge the status quo, and achieve greatness beyond measure.

In this chapter, we'll unravel the secrets of assembling a team of mavericks, misfits, and masterminds—individuals who bring their unique strengths and perspectives to the table, forging a synergy greater than the sum of its parts. But building a badass team isn't just about hiring the right people; it's about cultivating a culture of collaboration, innovation, and relentless pursuit of excellence. It's about fostering an environment where every member feels empowered to speak their truth, unleash their creativity, and push the boundaries of what's possible.

Consider the legendary leadership of Satya Nadella at Microsoft. When he took over as CEO, Nadella didn't just aim to maintain the status quo. He transformed Microsoft's corporate culture from a competitive, cutthroat environment to one that values collaboration, continuous learning, and empathy. This shift not only revitalized the company but also propelled it to new heights of innovation and success. Nadella's leadership exemplifies how nurturing a positive, inclusive culture can unlock the full potential of a team and drive exceptional results.

Great leaders command respect, not fear. They inspire a cult-like following by leading with integrity, authenticity, and vision. They understand that the path to legendary leadership is paved with the ability to make swift, sharp decisions while remaining adaptable and open to new ideas. This chapter will guide you through the essential qualities and strategies of legendary leadership, from commanding respect and inspiring your team to making decisive, impactful choices.

We'll dive deep into the art and science of team-building and leadership.

Command Respect, Not Fear

Great leaders command respect, not fear. Respect is earned through integrity, authenticity, and a clear vision. It's about demonstrating your unwavering commitment to your team's success and well-being. Show up consistently, make decisions transparently, and maintain a steadfast dedication to your values. Fear may force compliance, but respect inspires loyalty, motivation, and a sense of purpose. When your team respects you, they're not just following orders; they're rallying behind your vision with enthusiasm and dedication.

Creating an environment where people feel safe to take risks, voice their opinions, and grow is crucial. Encourage open dialogue, reward innovative thinking, and support your team in their professional journeys. Show them that you value their contributions and that you are invested in their success. This kind of environment fosters creativity, engagement, and high performance. Your team will follow you not because they have to, but because they believe in you and your vision.

Inspiring a Cult-Like Following

To inspire a cult-like following, you need to ignite passion and loyalty among your team. This goes beyond conventional leadership; it requires a profound connection with your team members. Share your vision compellingly, painting a vivid picture of the future that everyone can aspire to. Involve your team in shaping this vision, making them feel like co-creators in the journey. When people feel ownership over the direction of the company, their commitment and enthusiasm naturally increase.

Recognise and celebrate your team's achievements regularly. Be the leader who listens, understands, and empowers. Show genuine appreciation for their hard work and encourage a sense of pride in their contributions. Your investment in their growth and success will inspire them to go above and beyond, fuelling a collective drive toward achieving extraordinary goals. This deep-rooted loyalty and passion will create a cohesive, unstoppable force within your organisation.

Decision Making: Swift and Sharp

Legendary leaders are decisive. They understand that indecision is the enemy of progress. Making decisions quickly doesn't mean being reckless; it means being prepared and informed. Equip yourself with the necessary information, trust your intuition, and don't shy away from making tough calls. The ability to make swift, sharp decisions is a hallmark of effective leadership and a critical driver of success.

Be willing to pivot when new information arises, but avoid getting caught in analysis paralysis. Your decisiveness will instill confidence in your team and keep the momentum moving forward. When your team sees that you can make decisions under pressure and adapt as needed, they'll trust your leadership and feel secure in their roles. This trust and confidence are essential for maintaining high morale and productivity.

Leading with Empathy and Vision

Empathy is a powerful tool in leadership. Understanding and connecting with your team on a human level fosters a supportive and cohesive environment. Show genuine concern for their well-being, listen to their concerns, and provide support when needed. This empathy builds trust and loyalty, creating a strong bond between you and your team.

Combine empathy with a clear, compelling vision that everyone can rally around, and you've got a formula for unparalleled success.

Your vision should be ambitious yet attainable, inspiring your team to strive for greatness. Keep the lines of communication open and be receptive to feedback. This creates a dynamic where everyone feels valued and motivated to contribute their best, driving the organization forward with a unified purpose.

Cultivating a Culture of Excellence

A culture of excellence is built on high standards, continuous improvement, and recognition of achievements. Set the bar high and lead by example. Demonstrate the level of commitment and performance you expect from your team. Encourage your team to seek out learning opportunities and to always look for ways to improve. This mindset not only boosts morale but also drives your team to excel and innovate continually.

Celebrate wins, no matter how small, and use failures as learning experiences. Create an environment where mistakes are seen as opportunities for growth rather than setbacks. This approach fosters resilience, creativity, and a relentless pursuit of excellence. By cultivating this culture, you ensure that your team is always pushing the boundaries and striving for greatness.

Building Future Leaders

The mark of a true leader is not just their own success, but the success of those they mentor. Invest in developing future leaders within your team. Provide them with opportunities to take on new challenges, offer constructive feedback, and support their career growth. Building a pipeline of capable leaders ensures the long-term success and resilience of your organization.

Encourage your team members to develop their leadership skills and take on greater responsibilities. This not only prepares them for future roles but also empowers them to contribute more significantly to the organization's success. By focusing on building future leaders, you create a legacy of leadership excellence that will continue to drive your organisation forward long after you've moved on.

In conclusion, leading like a legend is about more than just managing a team; it's about inspiring, empowering, and developing them. By commanding respect, inspiring loyalty, making decisive choices, leading with empathy, cultivating a culture of excellence, and building future leaders, you can create an organisation that not only achieves success but also leaves a lasting impact. Embrace these principles and watch your leadership transform your team and drive your organisation to new heights.

Time to Level Up

Having explored the foundational elements of legendary leadership, commanding respect, inspiring loyalty, making decisive choices, leading with empathy, cultivating excellence, and building future leaders—it's time to delve deeper into the practical strategies that will elevate your leadership to the next level. Now that you understand the core principles, let's focus on the actionable tactics that will enable you to implement these concepts effectively within your organisation.

Building Trust and Credibility

Building trust and credibility is fundamental to effective leadership. Lead by example by demonstrating the values and behaviors you expect from your team. Act with integrity, transparency, and accountability in all your interactions. Communicate openly and honestly, fostering an environment where feedback is encouraged, concerns are addressed, and both successes and challenges are shared transparently. Trust and credibility are the bedrock upon which strong, cohesive teams are built.

Lead by Example

To truly lead by example, embody the qualities you wish to see in your team. This means showing up consistently, being reliable, and acting with integrity. Your actions should reflect your words, creating a strong foundation of trust. When your team sees you practicing what you preach, they will be more inclined to follow your lead and uphold the same standards.

Communicate Openly and Honestly

Open and honest communication is key to building trust. Foster a culture where feedback is welcomed and valued. Address concerns head-on and share both your successes and setbacks transparently. This openness not only builds trust but also encourages a culture of continuous improvement and collaboration.

Empowering Your Team

Empowerment is about entrusting your team with the authority and responsibility to make decisions and take ownership of their work. Delegate tasks strategically, showing confidence in your team's abilities. Encourage growth and development by providing opportunities for learning, skill-building, and career advancement. By investing in your team's development, you not only enhance their capabilities but also build a resilient, high-performing organisation.

Delegate Authority

Effective delegation involves more than just assigning tasks. It means entrusting your team members with the authority to make decisions and take ownership of their work. This empowerment boosts their confidence and engagement, leading to higher productivity and innovation.

Encourage Growth and Development

Invest in your team's growth by providing opportunities for learning and development. Offer training, mentorship, and career advancement opportunities. When your team members feel that their growth is a priority, they are more motivated and committed to contributing to the organisation's success.

Inspiring Vision and Purpose

To inspire a cult-like following, you need to ignite passion and loyalty among your team. This goes beyond conventional leadership; it requires a profound connection with your team members. Share your vision compellingly, painting a vivid picture of the future that everyone can aspire to. Involve your team in shaping this vision, making them feel like co-creators in the journey. When people feel ownership over the direction of the company, their commitment and enthusiasm naturally increase.

Articulate a Compelling Vision

Clearly communicate your vision for the future and the impact your business aims to achieve. Inspire passion and commitment by connecting individual roles to the broader mission. A compelling vision motivates your team to strive for greatness and stay aligned with the organisation's goals.

Align Goals and Values

Ensure that organisational goals align with the values and aspirations of your team members. Foster a sense of purpose that transcends individual tasks. When team members see how their work contributes to the larger vision, they are more engaged and motivated.

Leading with Empathy

Empathy is a powerful tool in leadership. Understanding and connecting with your team on a human level fosters a supportive and cohesive environment. Show genuine concern for their well-being, listen to their concerns, and provide support when needed. This empathy builds trust and loyalty, creating a strong bond between you and your team.

Show Empathy and Compassion

Understand and empathise with your team members' perspectives, feelings, and challenges. Show compassion and offer support during challenging times. Empathetic leadership creates a culture of trust and openness, encouraging team members to share their ideas and concerns freely.

Recognise and Appreciate

Acknowledge and appreciate the contributions of your team. Celebrate achievements and milestones to reinforce a culture of recognition. Recognition boosts morale and motivates team members to continue performing at their best.

Creating a Culture of Accountability

Accountability is crucial for maintaining high performance and achieving results. Set clear expectations, define goals, and establish standards of performance. Hold yourself and your team accountable for delivering results. Provide constructive feedback regularly, helping your team to grow and improve. By fostering a culture of accountability, you create a disciplined, goal-oriented environment that drives success.

Set Clear Expectations

Define clear goals, expectations, and standards of performance. Ensure that everyone understands their responsibilities and what is expected of them. Clear expectations create a sense of direction and purpose.

Provide Constructive Feedback

Offer timely and constructive feedback to help your team members grow and improve. Foster a culture where feedback is viewed as a valuable opportunity for development. Constructive feedback promotes continuous learning and improvement.

Resolving Conflict and Building Resilience

Address conflicts proactively and constructively. Encourage open dialogue and facilitate resolution through mediation or negotiation. Cultivate resilience within your team by fostering a positive and supportive environment. Encourage adaptive thinking and problem-solving in the face of challenges. By building resilience, you prepare your team to handle setbacks and emerge stronger.

Address Conflict Proactively

Handle conflicts and disagreements swiftly and constructively. Encourage open dialogue and facilitate resolution through mediation or negotiation. Proactive conflict resolution maintains a harmonious and productive work environment.

Cultivate Resilience

Build resilience within your team by fostering a positive and supportive environment. Encourage adaptive thinking and problem-solving in the face of challenges. Resilience enables your team to navigate setbacks and emerge stronger.

Leading Through Change and Uncertainty

Navigate change with confidence and clarity. Lead with decisiveness and provide reassurance during times of uncertainty. Communicate openly and guide your team through transitions. Stay calm under pressure and demonstrate resilience. Your composure and decisiveness will inspire trust and stability within your team.

Navigate Change Effectively

Lead with confidence during times of change and uncertainty. Provide reassurance, communicate openly, and guide your team through transitions. Effective change management minimises disruption and maintains morale.

Stay Calm Under Pressure

Maintain composure and resilience during challenging situations. Demonstrate confidence and decisiveness to inspire trust and stability. Your calm demeanour reassures your team and keeps them focused.

Continuous Learning and Improvement

Commit to continuous learning and improvement as a leader. Seek opportunities for personal and professional growth. Stay curious, embrace feedback, and adapt your leadership style based on insights and experiences. By continually developing your skills, you ensure that you remain effective and relevant as a leader.

Lead by Learning

Continuously seek opportunities to learn and grow as a leader. Stay curious, embrace feedback, and adapt your leadership style based on insights and experiences. Lifelong learning enhances your leadership effectiveness.

Invest in Decision-Making Skills

Develop your decision-making capabilities through training, mentorship, and continuous learning. Sharpen your analytical and critical thinking skills. Effective decision-making drives organisational success.

By commanding respect through trust, empowerment, and authenticity, you can cultivate a high-performing team that is motivated to achieve greatness. Leading like a legend isn't about wielding power—it's about inspiring and empowering others to unleash their full potential, driving collective success, and leaving a legacy of impactful leadership in the world of business. Take on task 5 to get to grips with your leadership style and identify improvements.

> **Task 5**
>
> Use the results of this assessment to reflect on your leadership style, identify areas for improvement, and develop a plan for enhancing your leadership effectiveness to lead like a legend.
>
> **Leadership Assessment Tool**: Assess your leadership style and strengths using this tool to command respect and inspire others.
>
> **Leadership Assessment Tool: Command Respect and Inspire Others**
>
> **Instructions:** Use this simple tool to assess your leadership style and strengths. Reflect on each statement and rate yourself based on your typical behaviours and approaches in leadership situations. Choose the rating that best represents your current leadership style (1 = Strongly Disagree, 2 = Disagree, 3 = Neutral, 4 = Agree, 5 = Strongly Agree).

1. **Vision and Purpose:**

    - I have a clear vision for the future of my team or organisation.

    1 | 2 | 3 | 4 | 5

2. **Communication Skills:**

    - I effectively communicate goals, expectations, and feedback to my team.

    1 | 2 | 3 | 4 | 5

3. **Decision-Making Ability:**

    - I make timely and informed decisions that benefit the team or organisation.

    1 | 2 | 3 | 4 | 5

4. **Empowerment and Delegation:**

    - I empower team members and delegate responsibilities effectively.

    1 | 2 | 3 | 4 | 5

5. **Adaptability and Resilience:**

    I adapt well to change and remain resilient in challenging situations.

    1 | 2 | 3 | 4 | 5

6. **Conflict Resolution:**

    - I handle conflicts and disagreements constructively and seek win-win solutions.

1 | 2 | 3 | 4 | 5

7. **Team Development:**
   - I invest in the professional development and growth of my team members.

   1 | 2 | 3 | 4 | 5

8. **Ethical Leadership:**
   - I demonstrate integrity and ethical behaviour in all aspects of leadership.

   1 | 2 | 3 | 4 | 5

9. **Innovation and Creativity:**
   - I encourage innovation and creativity within my team or organisation.

   1 | 2 | 3 | 4 | 5

10. **Accountability:**

    I hold myself and others accountable for results and outcomes.

    1 | 2 | 3 | 4 | 5

Scoring:

- Add up your scores for all 10 statements to determine your overall leadership assessment score.
- A higher score indicates stronger alignment with effective leadership practices.

Interpretation:

- 10-20: Opportunity for Growth - Identify areas for improvement and development in leadership skills.
- 21-30: Developing Leader - You demonstrate some leadership strengths, but there is room for growth.
- 31-40: Emerging Leader - You exhibit solid leadership qualities and have potential for further development.
- 41-50: Inspirational Leader - Congratulations! You possess strong leadership skills that command respect and inspire others.

Start compiling your notes here:

Chapter 6

Innovation & Disruption

Innovation is the lifeblood of every thriving business, and no one exemplifies this better than Steve Jobs, the visionary co-founder of Apple Inc. Jobs didn't just create products; he created entire industries with his relentless pursuit of innovation. From the iPod to the iPhone, Jobs disrupted the status quo and set trends that reshaped the way we live and work.

Here we'll draw inspiration from Jobs and other pioneering figures as we delve into the art of innovation and disruption. We'll explore how to cultivate a culture of creativity within your organisation, where every idea is welcomed, and no challenge is too daunting to overcome. Just as Jobs challenged the conventional wisdom of his time, we'll empower you to think outside the box and push the boundaries of what's possible.

But innovation isn't just about coming up with groundbreaking ideas; it's also about embracing technology to bring those ideas to life. Take, for instance, Reed Hastings, the co-founder, and CEO of Netflix, who transformed the way we consume entertainment by harnessing the power of streaming technology. Hastings's bold vision and unwavering commitment to innovation have made Netflix a global powerhouse in the entertainment industry.

So, strap in and prepare to embark on a journey of discovery and disruption. Whether you're a seasoned entrepreneur or a budding innovator, the lessons you'll learn in this chapter will empower you to innovate or get left behind, it's your choice. Get ready to unleash your creative genius and chart a course towards a future limited only by your imagination.

Becoming a Trendsetter

Becoming a trendsetter in business is about leading the way with vision, creativity, and a willingness to challenge the status quo. It's not enough to simply follow industry trends; true trendsetters create their own path, setting the pace for others to follow. This involves embracing innovation, taking calculated risks, and consistently pushing the boundaries of what's possible. By fostering a culture of creativity and experimentation within your organisation, you can cultivate an environment where new ideas flourish and groundbreaking solutions are developed.

A key aspect of being a trendsetter is thought leadership. By positioning yourself as an expert and a visionary, you can influence industry standards and inspire others to adopt your forward-thinking approaches. This involves not only staying informed about the latest developments in your field but also contributing to the conversation through public speaking, publishing insightful content, and engaging with your community. Strategic partnerships and collaborations can also play a crucial role in amplifying your impact, allowing you to leverage the strengths and insights of other innovators. Ultimately, becoming a trendsetter means being bold, staying ahead of the curve, and inspiring others to join you in driving the future of your industry.

Embrace a Forward-Thinking Mindset

Challenge the Status Quo: Break free from conventional thinking and challenge the status quo. Encourage a culture of curiosity, experimentation, and creative thinking within your organisation.

Anticipate Future Trends: Stay ahead of the curve by anticipating future trends and market shifts. Embrace emerging technologies and industry developments to position your business at the forefront.

Cultivate a Culture of Innovation

Empower Creative Talent: Invest in nurturing creative talent within your team. Encourage diverse perspectives, cross-functional collaboration, and risk-taking to fuel innovation.

Foster a Safe Environment for Experimentation: Create a safe space for experimentation and idea generation. Embrace failure as a stepping stone to success and celebrate learning from mistakes.

Drive Disruptive Change

Identify Untapped Opportunities: Explore unmet needs and untapped market segments. Look for gaps in the market where your innovation can make a significant impact.

Challenge Traditional Business Models: Disrupt traditional business models by offering unique value propositions and reimagining customer experiences. Embrace disruptive technologies to revolutionise your industry.

Lead with Vision and Purpose

Articulate a Bold Vision: Inspire your team with a bold and compelling vision for the future. Clearly communicate the purpose behind your innovation initiatives and rally support around your mission.

Align Innovation with Strategic Objectives: Ensure that innovation efforts are aligned with your overall business strategy and goals. Focus on initiatives that drive growth, differentiation, and competitive advantage.

Embrace Risk and Adaptability

Embrace Calculated Risks: Embrace calculated risks and pursue ambitious goals. Encourage a culture where calculated risk-taking is celebrated and rewarded.

Adapt to Change: Stay agile and adaptable in response to market dynamics and customer preferences. Embrace change as an opportunity for growth and evolution.

Continuous Learning and Improvement

Invest in Research and Development: Allocate resources to research and development to foster continuous innovation. Experiment with new technologies, processes, and business models.

Measure and Iterate: Establish metrics to measure the impact of innovation initiatives. Use feedback and data to iterate and refine your approach over time.

As a trendsetter in your industry, you can shape the future of business and establish your reputation as an innovative leader. Embrace a forward-thinking mindset, cultivate a culture of innovation, and drive disruptive change that propels your business towards new heights of success and relevance. Dare to challenge boundaries, defy expectations, and pioneer the next wave of industry evolution.

Disrupt or Be Disrupted: Staying Ahead of the Curve

Staying ahead of the curve requires a proactive approach to disruption. To thrive in competitive markets, businesses must embrace innovation and anticipate change before it arrives. This section delves into strategies for disrupting industries rather than being disrupted by them, ensuring your business remains at the forefront of innovation.

Monitor Industry Trends

Stay Informed: Keep a pulse on industry trends, emerging technologies, and shifts in consumer behaviour. Regularly scan the landscape for potential disruptors and opportunities.

Attend Conferences and Workshops: Participate in industry conferences, workshops, and networking events to connect with innovators and thought leaders. Gain insights into emerging trends and best practices.

Encourage a Culture of Innovation

Promote Idea Generation: Encourage employees at all levels to contribute ideas and suggestions for innovation. Create platforms for brainstorming and collaboration.

Reward Innovation: Recognise and reward innovative thinking and contributions. Incentivise risk-taking and experimentation to foster a culture of continuous improvement.

Invest in Research and Development

Allocate Resources: Dedicate resources to research and development (R&D) initiatives. Invest in exploring new technologies, processes, and business models that have the potential to disrupt markets.

Collaborate with Partners and Startups: Forge partnerships with startups, academia, and industry disruptors. Collaborate on joint ventures or pilot projects to leverage external expertise and insights.

Embrace Disruptive Technologies

Explore Emerging Technologies: Embrace disruptive technologies such as artificial intelligence (AI), blockchain, and Internet of Things (IoT) to innovate products, services, and operations.

Adopt Agile Practices: Implement agile methodologies to accelerate innovation cycles and respond quickly to changing market demands. Break down silos and promote cross-functional collaboration.

Anticipate Customer Needs

Customer-Centric Innovation: Understand evolving customer preferences and pain points. Anticipate future needs and develop solutions that exceed customer expectations.

Collect and Analyse Data: Leverage data analytics to gain actionable insights into customer behaviour and market trends. Use predictive analytics to anticipate future demands.

Be Willing to Disrupt Yourself

Being willing to disrupt yourself is a crucial mindset for sustained success. It means constantly questioning your own processes, products, and strategies, even when they seem to be working well. Complacency is the enemy of innovation, and by proactively seeking ways to improve and evolve, you can stay ahead of the competition and adapt to changing market demands. This requires a deep sense of self-awareness and the courage to acknowledge that there is always room for improvement. By embracing change and being open to new ideas, you create a dynamic environment where innovation thrives.

Disrupting yourself also involves taking calculated risks and being willing to pivot when necessary. This might mean abandoning a once-successful product line in favor of something more aligned with current trends or overhauling your business model to better meet the needs of your customers. It's about not getting too attached to the status quo and instead, fostering a culture of continuous learning and adaptability within your organisation. By regularly challenging your own assumptions and being willing to make bold changes, you not only future-proof your business but also inspire your team to think creatively and embrace change as a constant driver of growth and success.

Do forget to:

Challenge Existing Business Models: Continuously challenge and evolve your own business model. Be willing to cannibalise existing products or services to create new revenue streams.

Embrace Change as a Constant: Cultivate a mindset that embraces change and uncertainty. Encourage adaptability and resilience among your team members.

Lead with Vision and Courage

Communicate a Bold Vision: Inspire your team with a compelling vision for the future. Foster a sense of purpose and direction that aligns with disruptive innovation.

Take Calculated Risks: Encourage calculated risk-taking and experimentation. Create a safe environment where failure is viewed as a learning opportunity.

A proactive approach to disruption, businesses can position themselves as industry leaders and shape the future of their markets. Embrace innovation, cultivate a culture of continuous improvement, and be prepared to challenge the status quo to stay ahead of the curve. Disrupt or be disrupted—choose to lead the change and define the future of your industry.

Embracing Technology: Innovate or Die

In today's fast-evolving business landscape, embracing technology isn't just an option; it's a survival strategy. This section underscores the critical importance of integrating cutting-edge technology into every facet of your business to stay competitive and relevant. Innovate or die a stark but real choice that defines the modern market dynamics. As digital technologies transform industries at a breakneck pace, only those who adapt will thrive.

For businesses looking to future-proof themselves, the key lies in not just adopting technology, but in making it a core part of their innovation strategy. This means continually scouting for emerging tech trends, investing in new technologies that align with strategic business goals, and cultivating a culture that embraces change and technological advancement. By leveraging technology to optimise operations, enhance customer experiences, and create new value propositions, companies can not only survive but lead the charge in the redefinition of their industries.

Understanding the Digital Transformation

Acknowledge the Digital Imperative: Recognise that digital transformation is no longer optional it's essential for survival in today's competitive markets. Embrace technology as a catalyst for growth and evolution.

Adopt a Digital-First Mindset: Shift towards a digital-first approach in all aspects of your business operations, from customer engagement to supply chain management.

Harnessing the Power of Emerging Technologies

Explore Cutting-Edge Technologies: Stay abreast of emerging technologies such as artificial intelligence (AI), machine learning, cloud computing, and augmented reality (AR). Identify opportunities to integrate these technologies into your business processes.

Invest in Innovation Hubs: Establish innovation hubs or labs dedicated to experimenting with new technologies and developing disruptive solutions. Foster a culture of experimentation and collaboration.

Enhancing Customer Experience

Personalise Customer Interactions: Leverage data analytics and AI to personalise customer experiences. Anticipate individual needs and preferences to deliver tailored products and services.

Implement Omnichannel Strategies: Embrace omnichannel strategies that seamlessly integrate online and offline channels. Provide consistent and cohesive experiences across all touchpoints.

Optimising Operations and Efficiency

Automate Repetitive Tasks: Use robotic process automation (RPA) and AI-powered tools to automate mundane tasks and streamline workflows. Free up human resources for more strategic activities.

Improve Supply Chain Visibility: Implement blockchain technology to enhance supply chain transparency and traceability. Improve efficiency and reduce costs by optimising logistics and inventory management.

Driving Business Agility

Enable Remote Work: Embrace remote work and collaboration tools to enhance flexibility and productivity. Empower employees to work from anywhere while maintaining connectivity.

Adopt Agile Methodologies: Implement agile methodologies to accelerate project delivery and respond quickly to changing market dynamics. Foster a culture of adaptability and continuous improvement.

Mitigating Cybersecurity Risks

Prioritise Cybersecurity: Invest in robust cybersecurity measures to protect sensitive data and systems from cyber threats. Stay vigilant and proactive in identifying and addressing potential vulnerabilities.

Leadership in the Digital Age

Lead with Vision and Purpose: Inspire your team with a clear vision for digital transformation. Foster a culture of innovation, agility, and collaboration that embraces change.

Invest in Digital Literacy: Provide ongoing training and development in digital skills for employees at all levels. Build a workforce that is equipped to leverage technology effectively.

Businesses can position themselves for sustained growth and competitive advantage in a rapidly evolving marketplace. Innovate or die—choose to harness the power of technology to drive meaningful change, transform customer experiences, and future-proof your business for long-term success.

Remember that the pathway to becoming a trendsetter is not just about the big, explosive ideas it's about consistently stepping out of the comfort zone and challenging the status quo. It's about refusing to settle for good when you can achieve great. In this rapidly changing business landscape, staying ahead means embracing change as your only constant.

Innovators and disruptors are not born; they are made in the furnace of perseverance, creativity, and bold action. By applying the concepts and strategies discussed in this chapter, you're not just preparing to navigate the future, you're actively shaping it. Continue to leverage technology, harness creative thinking, and anticipate market shifts to keep your business not just running, but thriving.

So, as we turn the page on this chapter, let it not be the end of your innovation journey but the beginning of a bolder, more dynamic approach to business. Keep pushing the boundaries, keep asking the hard questions, and keep being the badass innovator you are destined to be.

Task 6

Use this Innovation Canvas to explore and develop innovative ideas that have the potential to disrupt your industry and position your business as a trendsetter. Collaborate with your team and stakeholders to leverage diverse perspectives and insights in the innovation process.

Innovation Canvas: Use this canvas to brainstorm and develop innovative ideas for becoming a trendsetter in your industry.

Innovation Canvas: Brainstorm and Develop Innovative Ideas

Instructions: Use this canvas to facilitate brainstorming sessions and develop innovative ideas for becoming a trendsetter in your industry. Fill out each section to explore, refine, and capture your innovative concepts.

1. **Problem or Opportunity:** Describe the specific problem or opportunity you want to address with your innovative idea.

2. **Target Audience:** Identify the target audience or customer segment for your innovation.

3. **Current Solutions and Limitations:** List existing solutions or approaches in the market and their limitations.

4. **Unique Value Proposition (UVP):** Define the unique value proposition of your innovation and how it addresses unmet needs.

5. **Key Features and Benefits:** Outline the key features and benefits of your innovation that differentiate it from existing solutions.

6. **Technology and Resources:** Identify technologies or resources required to develop and implement your innovation.

7. **Market Fit and Validation:** Assess the market fit and potential demand for your innovation through validation methods.

8. **Implementation Plan:** Define the steps and timeline for implementing your innovation from concept to launch.

9. **Potential Risks and Mitigation Strategies:** Identify potential risks or challenges associated with your innovation and develop mitigation strategies.

10. **Feedback and Iteration:** Plan for gathering feedback and iterating on your innovation based on user insights and market feedback.

Notes:

Chapter 7

The Ethics
Of Badassery

In business, it's easy to assume that to come out on top, you have to play dirty. But here's the twist in the tale: the real badasses know that strength lies in ethics. Take, for example, Anita Roddick, the founder of The Body Shop, who changed the beauty industry by prioritising ethical sourcing and sustainable practices. Roddick's commitment to ethical business not only set her brand apart but also inspired a movement towards corporate social responsibility.

This isn't about being soft; it's about being sustainably sharp. Ethical badassery is about defining your own rules within a framework that refuses to compromise on integrity. This chapter throws down the gauntlet, challenging you to navigate the murky waters of business with a moral compass as your guide. We'll dissect what it means to operate with transparency, accountability, and fairness, even when the pressure is on to cut corners.

Being ethical doesn't mean you lose your edge it means sharpening it against the whetstone of principled conduct. Here, ethics isn't just good karma; it's a competitive advantage. Prepare to explore how staying true to your values can not only elevate your business but also revolutionise your industry. Let's redefine what it means to be a badass by being as fiercely ethical as you are strategically astute.

Where to Draw the Line: Ethical Considerations

In the pursuit of badassery in business, navigating ethical considerations is paramount. This chapter delves into the complexities of ethical decision-making, exploring where to draw the line when faced with moral dilemmas and societal responsibilities.

Upholding Integrity and Values

Define Core Values: Establish a set of core values that guide your business practices. Commit to upholding integrity, honesty, and fairness in all interactions.

Lead by Example: Demonstrate ethical behaviour and decision-making as a leader. Set the tone for a culture of ethics and accountability within your organisation.

Balancing Profit and Principles

Avoid Short-Term Gains: Resist the temptation to prioritise short-term gains over long-term sustainability and ethical considerations. Align business objectives with ethical principles.

Consider Stakeholder Impact: Take into account the impact of your decisions on all stakeholders, including employees, customers, suppliers, and the broader community.

Navigating Gray Areas

Identify Ethical Gray Areas: Recognise situations that present ethical dilemmas or ambiguity. Seek clarity and guidance when faced with complex decisions.

Seek Counsel and Advice: Consult with trusted advisors, mentors, or ethics committees when navigating challenging ethical situations. Consider diverse perspectives before making decisions.

Transparency and Accountability

Practice Transparency: Communicate openly with stakeholders about business practices and decisions. Build trust through transparency and accountability.

Own Up to Mistakes: Take responsibility for errors or lapses in judgment. Demonstrate humility and a commitment to rectifying ethical breaches.

Addressing Social Responsibility

Corporate Social Responsibility (CSR): Embrace social responsibility by contributing positively to society. Engage in initiatives that promote environmental sustainability, diversity and inclusion, and community welfare.

Ethical Supply Chain: Ensure ethical practices throughout your supply chain. Partner with suppliers who adhere to fair labour standards and ethical sourcing practices.

Ethics in Innovation and Technology

Responsible Innovation: Consider ethical implications when developing and deploying new technologies. Prioritise safety, privacy, and societal well-being in innovation efforts.

Data Ethics: Safeguard customer data and respect privacy rights. Adhere to ethical data practices and comply with regulations governing data protection.

Continuous Ethical Reflection

Reflect and Adapt: Continuously reflect on ethical practices and adapt as needed. Stay informed about evolving ethical standards and industry norms.

Educate and Empower: Provide ethics training and resources to empower employees to make ethical decisions. Foster a culture of ethical awareness and accountability.

Navigating the ethical landscape requires vigilance, integrity, and a commitment to doing what is right even when faced with difficult choices. By embracing ethical considerations in business, you can build a reputation for trustworthiness, foster sustainable relationships, and contribute positively to society while pursuing your badass vision for success.

The Power of Transparency

Transparency is a cornerstone of ethical business practices, empowering leaders to build trust and credibility with stakeholders. This section explores the transformative impact of transparency in fostering ethical behaviour and enhancing organisational integrity.

Building Trust and Credibility

Open Communication: Embrace transparency in communication with employees, customers, investors, and other stakeholders. Share information openly and honestly, even when faced with challenging situations.

Accountability and Responsibility: Demonstrate accountability for decisions and actions. Take ownership of mistakes and communicate transparently about corrective measures.

Cultivating a Culture of Integrity

Lead by Example: Model ethical behaviour as a leader. Uphold high standards of integrity and inspire ethical conduct throughout the organisation.

Encourage Whistleblowing: Create channels for employees to report unethical behaviour without fear of retaliation. Encourage a culture of accountability and ethical awareness.

Enhancing Stakeholder Relationships

Customer Trust: Build customer trust through transparent business practices. Provide clear and accurate information about products, services, and pricing.

Investor Confidence: Foster investor confidence by maintaining transparency in financial reporting and governance. Disclose relevant information promptly and accurately.

Navigating Ethical Challenges

Ethical Decision-Making: Use transparency as a guide in ethical decision-making processes. Consider how decisions impact stakeholders and communicate openly about the rationale behind choices.

Addressing Controversies: Respond transparently to controversies or ethical concerns. Acknowledge issues, take appropriate action, and communicate transparently about steps taken to address them.

Adhering to Regulations and Standards

Compliance and Disclosure: Adhere to legal and regulatory requirements for transparency and disclosure. Keep stakeholders informed about compliance efforts and regulatory changes.

Ethical Supply Chain: Ensure transparency in supply chain practices. Collaborate with suppliers who uphold ethical standards and promote transparency in sourcing.

Embracing Ethical Innovation

Responsible Technology Use: Embrace ethical considerations in innovation and technology adoption. Prioritise data privacy, security, and responsible AI practices.

Data Protection: Protect customer data and privacy rights. Implement robust data protection measures and be transparent about data handling practices.

Continuous Improvement and Learning

Feedback and Adaptation: Solicit feedback from stakeholders and adapt transparency practices based on insights. Continuously improve transparency efforts to strengthen relationships and trust.

Education and Awareness: Educate employees and stakeholders about the importance of transparency in ethical business practices. Foster a shared commitment to integrity and transparency across the organisation.

By harnessing the power of transparency, businesses can foster a culture of integrity, build strong relationships with stakeholders, and navigate ethical challenges with confidence and credibility. Transparency is not just a buzzword it's a fundamental principle that underpins ethical leadership and contributes to sustainable success in the pursuit of badassery.

Social Responsibility: Badass with a Cause

In the realm of badass business leadership, social responsibility isn't just a checkbox—it's a powerful tool for creating positive impact and leaving a lasting legacy. This final section explores the transformative role of social responsibility in driving ethical business practices and becoming a force for good in the world.

Making a Meaningful Impact

Identify Causes that Matter: Align your business with causes that resonate with your values and mission. Champion initiatives that address social, environmental, or community needs.

Beyond Profit: Embrace a broader purpose beyond profit maximisation. Incorporate social impact goals into your business strategy and decision-making processes.

Engaging Stakeholders

Collaborate for Impact: Partner with NGOs, government agencies, and community organisations to amplify impact. Collaborative efforts can drive meaningful change and address systemic challenges.

Employee Engagement: Empower employees to participate in social responsibility initiatives. Encourage volunteerism, fundraising, or skills-based contributions to support causes they care about.

Driving Sustainable Change

Environmental Stewardship: Adopt sustainable practices to minimise environmental impact. Implement eco-friendly policies, reduce waste, and promote conservation efforts.

Ethical Sourcing and Fair Labour Practices: Ensure ethical sourcing throughout your supply chain. Support fair labour practices, human rights, and diversity and inclusion initiatives.

Building Trust and Reputation

Enhanced Brand Reputation: Earn trust and loyalty from customers by demonstrating commitment to social responsibility. Consumers increasingly favour brands that prioritise purpose-driven initiatives.

Investor Confidence: Attract socially responsible investors who value ethical practices and long-term sustainability. Socially responsible businesses are viewed as less risky and more resilient.

Measuring Impact and Accountability

Set Clear Goals and Metrics: Define measurable goals for social impact initiatives. Track progress, evaluate outcomes, and communicate results transparently.

Report on Impact: Publish annual sustainability reports or impact assessments. Share stories of success and lessons learned to inspire others and hold yourself accountable.

Inspiring a Movement

Lead by Example: Use your platform and influence to inspire others in the business community. Encourage industry-wide adoption of socially responsible practices.

Advocacy and Awareness: Advocate for policy changes that promote social and environmental responsibility. Raise awareness about pressing issues and mobilise support for collective action.

Continued Commitment to Badassery with a Cause

Embed Social Responsibility: Integrate social responsibility into your business DNA. Make it a core part of your brand identity and a driving force behind decision-making.

Leave a Lasting Legacy: Aspire to leave a positive legacy that extends beyond business success. Make a meaningful impact on society and future generations through your commitment to social responsibility.

With social responsibility as a badass with a cause, you can leverage your business platform to drive meaningful change, inspire others, and contribute to a more equitable and sustainable world. Transform your business into a force for good and redefine what it means to be a true badass leader in the 21st century.

As we wrap up Chapter 7, it's clear that the path of ethical badassery isn't just about avoiding pitfalls; it's about forging a legacy that stands the test of time. By embedding ethical considerations deeply into your business strategy, you not only ensure sustainability but also build a foundation of trust that attracts and retains top-tier talent, loyal customers, and dedicated stakeholders. This approach isn't about quick wins, it's about creating enduring success.

In the realm of badass business conduct, remember that every decision you make sends ripples through your entire organisation and beyond. Choosing the high road might be tougher, but it distinguishes you from the pack, setting a gold standard in an often cutthroat arena. As you move forward, let your ethical compass guide you in not just navigating challenges but in reshaping the landscape of your industry. Stand tall as the leader who not only rises to the top but lifts others up with integrity and courage. Keep your standards high and your actions bold, let's transform the face of business with badassery that's as righteous as it is ruthless.

Task 7

Use this Ethical Decision-Making Framework to guide your approach to ethical dilemmas and uphold ethical standards in your professional and personal life. Consider seeking advice from ethics experts or mentors when facing complex ethical challenges.

Ethical Decision-Making Framework: Navigate ethical dilemmas effectively with this practical framework for ethical considerations.

Ethical Decision-Making Framework

Instructions: Use this practical framework to navigate ethical dilemmas effectively and make informed decisions aligned with ethical considerations. Follow the steps below to evaluate ethical situations and determine the most ethical course of action.

1. **Identify the Ethical Issue:**
   - Clearly define the ethical issue or dilemma you are facing.

2. **Gather Relevant Information:**
   - Collect all pertinent facts, perspectives, and stakeholders involved in the situation.

3. **Consider Stakeholder Perspectives:**
   - Identify and assess the interests and perspectives of all affected stakeholders.

4. **Apply Ethical Principles:**
   - Evaluate the situation based on key ethical principles (e.g., honesty, fairness, respect for individuals).

5. **Explore Alternatives:**
   - Generate and assess potential courses of action that address the ethical issue.

6. **Evaluate Consequences:**
   - Predict and weigh the potential consequences (both positive and negative) of each alternative.

7. **Make a Decision:**
   - Select the course of action that best aligns with ethical principles and minimises harm.

8. **Implement and Monitor:**
   - Implement the decision and monitor outcomes to ensure ethical integrity and accountability.

Chapter 8

Personal Branding
You Are the Brand

A little earlier, we discussed building a "Social Savvy Brand Persona" and I even provided you with 15 top tips to get you started. So, why dedicate an entire chapter to personal branding? Let's dive in and find out.

Think of personal branding as your signature, your calling card, your indelible mark on the canvas of business. It's about finding your voice amidst the noise, standing tall amidst the sea of clones, and leaving an impression that's as unforgettable as a tattoo. Take, for instance, Sophia Amoruso, the founder of Nasty Gal, whose personal brand of unapologetic authenticity propelled her from an eBay seller to a fashion mogul. Amoruso's fearless approach to personal branding not only resonated with her audience but also set her apart in a crowded marketplace.

Here, we're ditching the cookie-cutter approach and diving headfirst into the art of crafting a persona that's as unique as you are. It's time to shake off the shackles of conformity and unleash the full force of your authenticity onto the business world. But beware, personal branding isn't for the faint of heart. It requires courage, audacity, and a willingness to embrace your quirks and idiosyncrasies. It's about owning your story, embracing your flaws, and turning them into strengths.

So, prepare to embark on a journey of self-discovery and self-expression that will redefine not just your brand, but your entire approach to business. Get ready to make waves, break moulds, and leave your mark on the world like only a true badass can.

Crafting a Persona That Sells

Standing out isn't just a luxury, it's a necessity. Crafting a persona that sells isn't about creating a facade or putting on a show; it's about authentically showcasing the best version of yourself in a way that captivates and inspires others. This part here is to peel back the layers of personal branding to reveal the essence of what makes you unique, compelling, and unforgettable.

Your personal brand isn't just a label, it's your promise to the world. It's the sum total of your values, your experiences, and your aspirations, distilled into a powerful narrative that speaks to your audience on a visceral level. By mastering the art of personal branding, you're not just selling a product or service; you're selling yourself the ultimate differentiator in a crowded marketplace. So, get ready to roll up your sleeves, dig deep into your authenticity, and craft a persona that not only sells but leaves a lasting legacy in the hearts and minds of those you touch.

Defining Your Unique Identity

Many people struggle with defining their unique identity because they either mimic others or fail to reflect on their own values and strengths. This can result in a generic and unmemorable brand. To correct this, take time for introspection and identify what truly sets you apart from others in your field. Reflect on your core values, strengths, and passions. Write them down and craft a distinct voice that aligns with your personality. Ensure your communication style resonates with your target audience. This process will help you build a strong, authentic brand that stands out.

Building Consistency and Cohesion

Inconsistency in visual identity and messaging is a common pitfall. Using different colours, fonts, and styles across various platforms can confuse your audience and dilute your brand. To address this, establish a cohesive visual identity. Choose a consistent colour palette, fonts, and imagery that reflect your brand's personality. Similarly, ensure your messaging is clear and cohesive. Communicate who you are and what you stand for in a way that is easy to understand. This consistency builds a unified brand identity that resonates with your audience and strengthens your brand's presence.

Authenticity and Credibility

Some people make the mistake of presenting a facade instead of their true selves, which can lead to a lack of trust and credibility. To correct this, embrace authenticity. Be genuine and transparent in all your interactions. Share your story in a compelling and relatable way, highlighting the experiences, challenges, and achievements that have shaped your professional journey. This transparency fosters trust and deeper connections with your audience. Remember, authenticity is essential for building a loyal following that believes in and supports your brand.

Differentiation and Positioning

Failing to differentiate yourself from others can result in your brand blending into the background. This often happens when people don't clearly define their niche or target audience. To correct this, define your target audience and niche market clearly. Tailor your brand message to address their specific needs and interests. Position yourself as the go-to expert in your area by emphasising your unique skills, expertise, and perspectives. Highlight your Unique Selling Proposition (USP) in a clear and compelling way. This will help you attract and retain an audience that values what you uniquely offer.

Strategic Networking and Visibility

Many individuals fail to leverage digital platforms effectively or network strategically. This can limit their visibility and growth opportunities. To correct this, build a strong online presence. Maintain an updated LinkedIn profile, create a professional website, and engage actively on relevant social media channels. Network strategically by cultivating meaningful relationships with industry peers, influencers, and potential collaborators. Attend networking events, join professional associations, and engage in conversations that enhance your professional network. These actions will expand your reach and help you connect with a broader audience.

Consistent Brand Evolution

Stagnation is a common issue when people fail to adapt to changing trends and technologies. To avoid this, commit to consistent brand evolution. Continuously evolve your personal brand to stay relevant. Adapt to emerging trends and technologies to keep your brand fresh and engaging. Regularly seek feedback from peers, mentors, and your audience to refine your personal brand. Embrace constructive criticism as an opportunity for growth and continuous improvement. By doing so, you ensure your brand not only stands out but also endures in the competitive business landscape.

Course Correction Actions:

1. Self-Assessment: Regularly reflect on your values, strengths, and unique qualities. Write them down and revisit them to ensure your brand remains true to who you are.

2. Brand Audit: Conduct a thorough review of your visual and messaging consistency across all platforms. Make necessary adjustments to ensure cohesion.

3. Authentic Storytelling: Practice sharing your authentic story. Highlight both successes and failures to build trust and relatability with your audience.

4. Market Research: Define and refine your target audience and niche market. Adjust your messaging to better address their needs and interests.

5. Digital Presence: Ensure all your online profiles are updated and consistent. Engage actively on social media and professional networks.

6. Networking Plan: Develop a strategic networking plan. Identify key events, associations, and individuals that align with your goals and actively engage with them.

7. Feedback Loop: Create a system for regular feedback from peers, mentors, and your audience. Use this feedback to make continuous improvements to your brand.

8. Trend Monitoring: Stay informed about industry trends and technological advancements. Adapt your brand strategy to incorporate these changes and maintain relevance.

By recognising and addressing these common mistakes, you can refine your personal brand and enhance your professional presence. Taking these corrective actions will help you build a strong, authentic, and enduring brand that resonates with your audience and supports your growth.

Authenticity vs. The Ideal Self: Striking a Balance

Throughout this book, we emphasise authenticity frequently. Why? Because people often forget that authenticity is one of the foundational elements of success. Without it, you may achieve some success, but you'll never reach your full potential.

Authenticity reigns supreme but so does the allure of the ideal self. Striking the delicate balance between these two forces is a challenge that every badass entrepreneur must face head-on. In this section, we delve into the intricacies of navigating this tightrope walk, ensuring that you remain true to your core while strategically shaping a persona that elevates your brand and connects with your audience on a profound level.

Authenticity is your north star, guiding every decision and action you take in the realm of personal branding. It's the raw, unfiltered essence of who you are the soul of your brand that resonates with authenticity and integrity. But authenticity alone isn't enough; in today's competitive landscape, you also need to project an image that inspires and motivates, the aspirational "ideal self" that represents the best version of who you aspire to be.

So, how do you strike this delicate balance? By staying rooted in your values and beliefs while embracing growth and evolution. It's about being transparent about your journey, acknowledging your flaws and imperfections, and showcasing your authenticity in every interaction. At the same time, it's about setting audacious goals, stretching beyond your comfort zone, and daring to become the person you've always dreamed of being. By embracing both authenticity and the ideal self, you create a personal brand that's not just compelling it's downright irresistible.

However, along with the triumphs of building a strong personal brand, you will inevitably face challenges from naysayers, critics, and trolls. Navigating these attacks requires a strategic approach to maintain your integrity and protect your brand. In the next section, we will explore how to handle negative feedback, defend against attacks on your image and ideals, and deal with trolls effectively. By mastering these skills, you can fortify your brand against adversity and continue to thrive in the digital landscape.

Negatives and Attacks

We know that having a brand and living our brand is important. However, on this journey, you will encounter people who are jealous, don't understand your vision, or believe you don't deserve your success. These individuals may want to see you fail, metaphorically speaking. As you carve out your unique space in the digital landscape, you'll inevitably encounter both positive and negative feedback. While praise can boost your confidence and validate your efforts, negative feedback, attacks on your image or ideals, and trolls can pose significant challenges. How you handle these situations can significantly impact your brand's perception and your personal resilience.

Dealing with Negative Feedback

Negative feedback, while often difficult to accept, can be a valuable source of learning and growth. When faced with criticism, it's essential to approach it with an open mind and a constructive attitude. First, evaluate the feedback objectively. Determine whether the criticism is valid and if there are actionable insights you can take from it. Avoid responding impulsively; instead, take the time to reflect on the feedback and respond thoughtfully.

Thank the person for their input, even if it stings. Acknowledging feedback shows maturity and a willingness to improve, which can enhance your credibility and respect among your audience. If the feedback highlights a genuine flaw or mistake, admit it openly and outline the steps you are taking to address it. This transparency demonstrates accountability and can turn a potentially negative situation into an opportunity to strengthen your brand.

Handling Attacks on Your Image or Ideals

When someone attacks your image or ideals, it can feel deeply personal and unsettling. These attacks often come from a place of misunderstanding or malice. It's crucial to remain calm and composed in such situations. Begin by assessing the situation: Is the attack based on a misunderstanding that can be clarified, or is it a deliberate attempt to undermine you?

For misunderstandings, provide a clear and measured response that clarifies your position. Use this as an opportunity to reaffirm your values and ideals, demonstrating consistency and integrity in your beliefs. If the attack is a deliberate attempt to damage your reputation, it may be best to address it briefly and then move on, avoiding prolonged engagement that could escalate the situation.

In some cases, it might be appropriate to involve a third party, such as a mentor or a PR professional, to help manage the situation effectively. Showing resilience in the face of attacks and standing firm in your beliefs can ultimately strengthen your personal brand.

Managing Trolls

Trolls are a unique and particularly disruptive challenge in the digital world. These individuals seek to provoke, upset, and derail conversations with inflammatory and irrelevant comments. The first rule in dealing with trolls is not to feed them. Engaging with trolls often only encourages more disruptive behaviour and draws you into pointless, energy-draining exchanges.

Instead, focus on maintaining the integrity of your brand space. Use platform tools to moderate comments and, where necessary, block or report users who persistently troll. Ensure your community guidelines are clear, and enforce them consistently to maintain a respectful and constructive environment.

When responding is necessary, keep your replies short, factual, and devoid of emotion. By not giving trolls the reaction they seek, you maintain control of the conversation and demonstrate your professionalism. Additionally, leverage the support of your community. Encouraging positive, supportive interactions can drown out the negativity and reinforce a sense of solidarity among your followers.

Dealing with negative feedback, attacks on your image or ideals, and trolls is an inevitable part of maintaining a strong personal brand. By approaching these challenges with composure, clarity, and a constructive mindset, you can turn potential setbacks into opportunities for growth. Showcasing your resilience, integrity, and professionalism in the face of adversity will not only protect your brand but also enhance its reputation and strength in the long run.

> **Task 8**
>
> Use this Personal Branding Blueprint to create a cohesive and compelling brand persona that enhances your visibility, credibility, and authenticity. Regularly review and update your blueprint to adapt to changing trends and audience preferences.
>
> **Personal Branding Blueprint**: Craft your unique brand persona using this blueprint template to enhance visibility and authenticity.

Personal Branding Blueprint

Instructions: Use this blueprint template to craft your unique brand persona and enhance visibility and authenticity in personal branding. Complete each section to define key elements of your personal brand and create a cohesive brand strategy.

1. **Brand Identity:**

    - Define your brand identity in a few words (e.g., innovative, trustworthy, visionary).

2. **Brand Vision:**

    - Clarify your long-term vision and goals for your personal brand.

3. **Target Audience:**

    - Identify your target audience or ideal followers (e.g., industry professionals, aspiring entrepreneurs).

4. **Unique Selling Proposition (USP):**

    - Define what sets you apart from others in your field or industry.

5. **Brand Messaging:**
    - Craft a compelling brand message that resonates with your audience.

6. **Visual Identity:**
    - Choose visual elements (e.g., logo, colour scheme, typography) that reflect your brand personality.

7. **Content Strategy:**
    - Outline your content strategy for sharing valuable insights, stories, and expertise.

8. **Platforms and Channels:**
    - Identify the primary platforms and channels (e.g., social media, blogs, podcasts) to showcase your brand.

9. **Engagement Plan:**
    - Develop a plan for engaging with your audience and building meaningful connections.

10. **Authenticity Check:**
    - Assess the authenticity of your brand persona and ensure alignment with your values and personality.

Start crafting your plan here:

Chapter 9

Build and Leading
Badass Teams

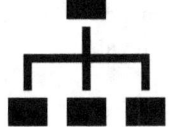

Building and Leading Badass Teams

This is where success isn't just measured by individual accomplishments, but by the collective power of a badass team. We're about to embark on a journey into the heart of leadership, where the true magic happens; building teams that defy the odds, challenge the status quo, and achieve greatness beyond measure.

Consider the example of Sara Blakely, the founder of Spanx, who revolutionised the undergarment industry with her innovative shapewear products. Blakely's success was not just a result of her individual brilliance but also her ability to assemble a team of diverse talents and personalities. She understood the importance of hiring individuals who shared her vision and drive, creating a culture of innovation and collaboration that propelled Spanx to global success.

Here, we'll unravel the secrets of assembling a team of mavericks, misfits, and masterminds, individuals who bring their unique strengths and perspectives to the table, forging a synergy that's greater than the sum of its parts. But building a badass team isn't just about hiring the right people; it's about cultivating a culture of collaboration, innovation, and relentless pursuit of excellence. It's about fostering an environment where every member feels empowered to speak their truth, unleash their creativity, and push the boundaries of what's possible.

So, tighten the boot laces and prepare to dive deep into the art and science of team-building and leadership. Whether you're a seasoned entrepreneur or a budding business tycoon, the lessons you'll learn in this chapter will not only transform the way you lead but also pave the way for unprecedented success in your business ventures. Get ready to unleash the full potential of your team and lead them to heights you never thought possible. Because when you lead with badassery, anything is achievable

Hiring Mavericks: Talent Acquisition for Innovators

Hiring mavericks isn't just a strategy, it's a necessity. When it comes to building your dream team, you need more than just skilled individuals; you need trailblazers, rebels, and visionaries who aren't afraid to shake things up and break the mould. In this section, we'll explore the art of talent acquisition for innovators, uncovering the secrets to identifying, attracting, and recruiting the kind of game-changers who can take your business to new heights.

Gone are the days of hiring based solely on qualifications and experience. Today, it's all about finding individuals who possess that special spark, the innate drive and passion to challenge the status quo and pioneer new paths forward. From unconventional interview techniques to out-of-the-box recruitment strategies, we'll show you how to cast your net wide and reel in the kind of talent that can truly transform your organisation. So, buckle up and prepare to embark on a journey of discovery as we dive deep into the world of hiring mavericks. Because when you surround yourself with innovators and disruptors, there's no limit to what you can achieve.

Think Beyond the CV: Don't settle for cookie-cutter resumes. Look for candidates who bring a spark of originality and a thirst for innovation to the table.

Spot the Rebels: Seek out individuals who aren't afraid to challenge conventions and think outside the box. Mavericks are the ones who will shake things up and propel your team forward.

Embrace Unconventional Experience: Value diverse backgrounds and unconventional career paths. The right maverick may not fit the traditional mould but brings invaluable perspectives and skills.

Passion over Perfection: Prioritise passion and drive over flawless qualifications. Look for candidates who are hungry to make a difference and unafraid to take risks.

Culture Fit with a Twist: Focus on cultural alignment but leave room for diverse personalities. Mavericks might not fit the typical "company culture" and that's okay—they'll shape it into something extraordinary.

By focusing on hiring mavericks, you're not just building a team—you're assembling a squad of fearless innovators ready to disrupt industries and challenge the status quo. Embrace the unconventional, harness the power of diversity, and watch your team redefine what's possible in the world of business.

Cultivating a Culture of Challenge and Triumph

In a badass team, challenges aren't roadblocks, they're opportunities for triumph. Cultivating a culture that thrives on overcoming obstacles and celebrating victories is essential for fostering resilience and driving innovation.

Embrace the Growth Mindset: Encourage a growth mindset where failures are viewed as learning experiences. Encourage team members to embrace challenges and persist in the face of setbacks.

Set Ambitious Goals: Challenge your team with ambitious yet achievable goals. Inspire them to stretch beyond their comfort zones and strive for greatness.

Promote Collaboration: Foster a collaborative environment where team members support each other and share diverse perspectives. Collaboration sparks creativity and propels the team towards success.

Celebrate Small Wins: Recognise and celebrate incremental successes along the way. Acknowledge individual and collective achievements to keep morale high and motivation strong.

Encourage Innovation: Create space for experimentation and innovation. Encourage team members to propose new ideas, take calculated risks, and explore unconventional solutions.

Lead by Example: Demonstrate resilience and determination as a leader. Show your team that challenges are opportunities to shine and inspire them with your own tenacity.

Provide Support and Resources: Equip your team with the tools, resources, and support they need to tackle challenges effectively. Remove obstacles and empower them to thrive.

Emphasise Learning and Growth: Foster a culture of continuous improvement and professional development. Encourage ongoing learning and skill-building among team members.

Adapt and Pivot: Be adaptable in the face of challenges or changing circumstances. Encourage flexibility and agility in problem-solving approaches.

Cultivating a culture of challenge and triumph empowers your team to conquer obstacles, surpass expectations, and achieve extraordinary results. Embrace the journey of growth, celebrate successes, and transform challenges into stepping stones towards greatness. Together, your team will embody resilience, innovation, and unwavering determination—the hallmarks of a truly badass crew.

Delegation and Empowerment: Scaling Your Influence

Delegation and empowerment aren't just strategies, they're superpowers that can elevate your influence to new heights. Delegation isn't just about offloading tasks; it's about entrusting your team members with the responsibility and autonomy to take ownership of their work and make meaningful contributions to the organisation. Likewise, empowerment isn't just about giving lip service to employee engagement, it's about fostering a culture of trust, respect, and accountability that empowers individuals to unleash their full potential and drive results.

So, get ready to unleash the full power of delegation and empowerment as we explore the strategies, tactics, and mindset shifts needed to scale your influence and lead your team to greatness. Whether you're a seasoned executive or a rising star in the business world, the lessons you'll learn in this section will empower you to build a team that's not just capable but unstoppable.

Assign Responsibilities Strategically: Delegate tasks based on individual strengths, skills, and developmental goals. Empower team members by entrusting them with meaningful responsibilities that align with their expertise and aspirations.

Clarify Expectations and Goals: Clearly communicate expectations, desired outcomes, and timelines when delegating tasks. Ensure alignment with overall team objectives to maintain focus and direction.

Provide Autonomy and Decision-Making Authority: Empower team members to make decisions within their scope of responsibilities. Encourage autonomy and ownership over tasks to foster confidence and initiative.

Offer Guidance and Support: Be available to provide guidance, advice, and resources when needed. Support team members in their roles and offer constructive feedback to facilitate growth and development.

Encourage Innovation and Creativity: Create an environment that encourages innovation and creativity. Allow team members to explore new ideas and approaches, empowering them to contribute to strategic initiatives.

Establish Clear Communication Channels: Foster open and transparent communication within the team. Establish regular check-ins, feedback sessions, and forums for sharing ideas and progress updates.

Celebrate Achievements and Successes: Recognise and celebrate individual and collective achievements. Highlight the impact of empowered team members and their contributions to team goals.

Delegate Authority, Not Just Tasks: Delegate decision-making authority along with tasks. Empower team members to take ownership of projects and initiatives, fostering a sense of accountability and pride.

Promote a Culture of Continuous Improvement: Encourage continuous learning and development. Provide opportunities for skills enhancement, training, and mentorship to empower team members to excel in their roles.

Lead by Example: Demonstrate delegation and empowerment through your own actions. Delegate responsibilities to demonstrate trust in your team and model the behaviour you wish to see.

Monitor Progress and Offer Support: Stay informed about project progress and offer support as needed. Address challenges proactively and provide resources to overcome obstacles.

Delegation and empowerment are not just about distributing tasks—they are about empowering individuals to contribute meaningfully to the team's success. By fostering a culture of delegation and empowerment, you can scale your influence as a leader, build a high-performing team, and achieve exceptional outcomes collectively.

It's clear that building and leading a badass team isn't just about assembling a group of talented individuals, it's about cultivating a tribe of like-minded warriors who are united in their pursuit of excellence. It's about fostering a culture of collaboration, trust, and mutual respect, where every member feels empowered to contribute their best work and push the boundaries of what's possible.

But the journey doesn't end here. As you venture forth into the world of business leadership, remember that your team is only as strong as its leader. It's up to you to set the tone, lead by example, and inspire greatness in every member of your team. By embracing the principles of badassery in leadership, courage, authenticity, and unwavering determination, you'll not only unlock the full potential of your team but also pave the way for enduring success in your business endeavours.

So, go forth with confidence, knowing that you have the knowledge, skills, and mindset to build and lead a team of true badasses. Embrace the challenges, celebrate the victories, and never lose sight of the incredible impact you can make when you lead with passion and purpose. The world is yours for the taking, so go out there and build the team of your dreams.

Task 9

Team Dynamics Diagnostic Tool: Assess team dynamics and identify areas for improvement in cultivating a culture of challenge and triumph.

Team Dynamics Diagnostic Tool

Instructions: Use this diagnostic tool to assess team dynamics and identify areas for improvement in cultivating a culture of challenge and triumph within your team. Evaluate each statement and rate your team's performance based on your observations and experiences (1 = Strongly Disagree, 2 = Disagree, 3 = Neutral, 4 = Agree, 5 = Strongly Agree).

1. **Clear Goals and Objectives:**
    - The team has clear and well-defined goals that align with organisational objectives.

        1 | 2 | 3 | 4 | 5

2. **Open Communication:**
    - Team members communicate openly and transparently, sharing ideas and feedback freely.

        1 | 2 | 3 | 4 | 5

3. **Collaborative Environment:**
    - The team collaborates effectively, leveraging diverse skills and perspectives.

        1 | 2 | 3 | 4 | 5

4. **Resilience and Adaptability:**
    - Team members demonstrate resilience and adaptability in the face of challenges.

        1 | 2 | 3 | 4 | 5

5. **Innovation and Creativity:**
    - The team encourages innovation and creativity, exploring new ideas and solutions.

        1 | 2 | 3 | 4 | 5

6. **Celebration of Success:**
    - Achievements and milestones are celebrated, fostering a culture of triumph.

        1 | 2 | 3 | 4 | 5

7. **Empowerment and Accountability:**

    - Team members are empowered to make decisions and take ownership of their work.

    1 | 2 | 3 | 4 | 5

8. **Constructive Conflict Resolution:**

    - The team resolves conflicts constructively, focusing on mutual understanding and resolution.

    1 | 2 | 3 | 4 | 5

9. **Continuous Improvement:**

    - The team embraces a growth mindset, seeking opportunities for learning and development.

    1 | 2 | 3 | 4 | 5

10. **Trust and Mutual Respect:**

    - Trust and mutual respect are established among team members.

    1 | 2 | 3 | 4 | 5

Scoring:

- Calculate the average score for each statement based on your team's ratings.

- Higher scores indicate stronger team dynamics and a more conducive environment for cultivating a culture of challenge and triumph.

Interpretation:

- 10-20: Opportunity for Improvement - Identify areas for enhancement and development in team dynamics.

- 21-30: Developing Team - Your team demonstrates some positive dynamics but has room for growth.

- 31-40: High-Performing Team - Congratulations! Your team exhibits strong dynamics conducive to success and innovation.

Use the results of this Team Dynamics Diagnostic Tool to initiate discussions, implement improvements, and foster a culture of challenge and triumph within your team.

Chapter 10

Crisis Management

Crises are not just inevitable, they're opportunities for badassery. Take a page from the playbook of Elon Musk, the visionary entrepreneur behind SpaceX and Tesla. When faced with seemingly insurmountable challenges, Musk has time and again demonstrated his ability to turn adversity into advantage, transforming setbacks into monumental achievements. From overcoming rocket launch failures to revolutionising the electric car industry, Musk's fearless approach to crisis management is a testament to the power of resilience and innovation in the face of adversity.

Forget everything you thought you knew about crisis management. In this section, we're not just talking about weathering the storm; we're talking about harnessing its power to propel you to new heights of success. From strategic decision-making to tactical execution, we'll show you how to navigate the treacherous waters of crisis with finesse and flair. Just as Musk has done time and again, it's time to seize the moment, embrace the chaos, and turn adversity into opportunity.

So, prepare to embrace the chaos, because there's no such thing as a crisis, only opportunities in disguise. It's time to unleash your inner warrior, face adversity head-on, and emerge victorious on the other side. Are you ready to turn your greatest challenges into your greatest triumphs?

Handling High-Pressure Situations with Finesse

In the fast-paced world of business, crisis management is a critical skill that separates the ordinary from the extraordinary. This chapter explores the art of handling high-pressure situations with finesse, equipping you with strategies to navigate challenges and emerge stronger than ever.

Embrace the Calm Amidst Chaos: In times of crisis, maintaining a calm and composed demeanour is essential. Cultivate resilience and clarity of mind to make informed decisions under pressure.

Strategic Decision-Making: Learn to prioritise and make strategic decisions swiftly during crises. Focus on mitigating risks and protecting key stakeholders while maintaining a long-term perspective.

Effective Communication: Master the art of clear and transparent communication during crises. Keep stakeholders informed, address concerns promptly, and demonstrate leadership through your words and actions.

Build a Resilient Team: Foster a culture of preparedness and adaptability within your team. Equip them with the skills and resources needed to respond effectively to unexpected challenges.

Learn from Adversity: View crises as learning opportunities. Identify lessons learned and use them to strengthen your organisation's crisis response strategies for the future.

Handling high-pressure situations with finesse requires a blend of strategic thinking, effective communication, and unwavering leadership. By mastering crisis management skills, you can navigate challenges confidently and lead your team through adversity towards success.

Turning Disasters into Opportunities

In business, crises often present hidden opportunities for growth and innovation. This section explores how to leverage adversity to your advantage and transform disasters into strategic opportunities.

Embrace Adaptive Leadership: During crises, adopt an adaptive leadership style that empowers you to pivot and capitalise on emerging opportunities. Be open to unconventional approaches and agile decision-making.

Identify Silver Linings: Look for silver linings amid adversity. Identify areas of potential improvement, innovation, or efficiency that can emerge from crisis-driven changes.

Innovate Under Pressure: Encourage innovation and creativity during turbulent times. Challenge your team to think outside the box and explore new solutions that address evolving market demands.

Reevaluate Business Models: Use crises as an opportunity to reevaluate and refine your business model. Identify weaknesses and inefficiencies, and implement strategic changes to enhance resilience and competitiveness.

Explore New Markets or Offerings: Explore diversification opportunities in response to changing market dynamics. Consider entering new markets or developing innovative products/services to meet emerging needs.

Adopt a Growth Mindset: Cultivate a growth mindset that views setbacks as temporary obstacles. Encourage continuous learning and adaptation to foster resilience and perseverance.

Engage Stakeholders Strategically: Leverage crisis situations to strengthen relationships with key stakeholders. Demonstrate transparency, integrity, and responsiveness to build trust and loyalty.

Invest in Strategic Initiatives: Allocate resources towards strategic initiatives that position your organisation for long-term success. Invest in technology, talent development, or infrastructure upgrades that enhance resilience and agility.

Communicate Vision and Purpose: Inspire confidence and rally your team around a shared vision during turbulent times. Communicate the purpose behind your actions and instil a sense of collective purpose.

Monitor Market Trends: Stay vigilant and monitor market trends during and after crises. Identify emerging opportunities and adapt your strategies accordingly to stay ahead of the curve.

Turning disasters into opportunities requires foresight, adaptability, and a proactive approach to crisis management. By reframing challenges as catalysts for growth and innovation, you can position your organisation to thrive in an ever-changing business landscape.

The Resilience Playbook: Comeback Stronger

Resilience isn't just a trait, it's a freakin superpower. In the face of adversity, setbacks, and unforeseen challenges, it's the resilience playbook that separates the contenders from the champions. Crafting a playbook isn't just about waiting out for the next sunny sky; it's about turning adversity into opportunity, chaos into clarity, and setbacks into stepping stones towards greatness.

So, how do you build a resilience playbook that's worthy of the badassery required to navigate the turbulent waters of crisis management? It starts with a mindset, a mindset of unwavering determination, relentless optimism, and unshakeable resolve. It's about embracing the challenges, facing them head-on, and refusing to let setbacks define your destiny.

But resilience isn't just about bouncing back; it's about bouncing back stronger than ever before. It's about learning from the past, adapting to the present, and shaping the future with unwavering confidence and courage. So, as you craft your resilience black book, remember that the journey isn't always smooth, but it's the bumps in the road that make the victory that much sweeter. My advice, embrace the chaos, and get ready to come back stronger than ever before. After all, there is no such thing as defeat—only opportunities for epic comebacks.

Assess Vulnerabilities: Conduct a comprehensive assessment of your organisation's vulnerabilities and risk exposure. Identify areas that require strengthening to enhance resilience.

Develop Contingency Plans: Create contingency plans for various crisis scenarios, outlining clear protocols and response strategies. Ensure that key stakeholders are familiar with their roles and responsibilities.

Invest in Risk Mitigation: Allocate resources towards risk mitigation efforts, such as cybersecurity measures, supply chain diversification, and crisis communication strategies.

Prioritise Employee Wellbeing: Place a strong emphasis on employee wellbeing and mental health. Implement support programmes and initiatives to help employees cope with stress and uncertainty.

Establish Crisis Communication Protocols: Develop robust communication protocols to keep stakeholders informed during crises. Maintain transparency and clarity in your messaging to build trust and credibility.

Learn from Past Experiences: Continuously evaluate and learn from past crisis experiences. Use insights gained to refine your resilience strategies and improve preparedness for future challenges.

Foster Organisational Agility: Cultivate an agile organisational culture that embraces change and adapts quickly to shifting circumstances. Encourage innovation and flexibility in decision-making.

Build Strategic Partnerships: Collaborate with strategic partners and industry peers to share resources, insights, and best practices for crisis management. Leverage collective expertise to strengthen resilience.

Invest in Continuous Improvement: Foster a culture of continuous improvement and adaptation. Encourage feedback, innovation, and iteration to evolve your resilience playbook over time.

Lead with Resilience: As a leader, embody resilience in your actions and decisions. Demonstrate unwavering resolve and determination to overcome challenges and inspire confidence in your team.

By implementing a resilience playbook grounded in proactive risk management, robust communication, and adaptive leadership, you can navigate crises with confidence and come back stronger. Embrace resilience as a strategic advantage and empower your organisation to thrive in the face of adversity.

Strategic Alliances: Choosing the Right Partners

Strategic alliances serve as the cornerstone of successful international expansion. Choosing the right partners isn't just a matter of convenience, it's a strategic imperative that can make or break your foray into new markets. When it comes to forging alliances, it's crucial to seek out partners who not only complement your strengths but also share your vision and values.

But finding the perfect match isn't always easy. It requires careful consideration, thorough due diligence, and a keen eye for mutual benefit. Look for partners who bring unique resources, expertise, and market insights to the table, those who can help you navigate the complexities of international business and unlock new opportunities for growth and expansion.

Above all, prioritise trust, transparency, and alignment of interests. Choose partners who are committed to your success and who are willing to invest time, effort, and resources into building a mutually beneficial relationship. By forging strong alliances with trusted allies, you'll not only expand your global footprint but also lay the foundation for long-term success and prosperity in the fiercely competitive world of international business. Here's how to choose the right partners for your international endeavours:

Align with Shared Goals and Values: Look for partners who share similar goals, values, and vision for business expansion. Ensure alignment in long-term objectives and commitment to mutual success.

Complementary Capabilities: Seek partners with complementary capabilities and strengths that enhance your competitive advantage in international markets. Identify areas of synergy where collaboration can drive innovation and market penetration.

Market Knowledge and Expertise: Prioritise partners with deep market knowledge and expertise in target regions. Choose allies who understand local regulations, consumer behaviours, and market dynamics to navigate complexities effectively.

Established Reputation and Credibility: Partner with reputable organisations or industry leaders known for their credibility and integrity. Leverage their brand reputation and network to build trust and credibility in new markets.

Compatibility and Trust: Build partnerships based on mutual trust, transparency, and compatibility. Establish clear communication channels and governance structures to foster collaboration and resolve potential conflicts.

Risk-sharing and Resource Allocation: Evaluate risk-sharing and resource allocation strategies with potential partners. Explore mutual investment opportunities and shared responsibilities to optimise operational efficiency and minimise risks.

Cultural Compatibility: Consider cultural compatibility and alignment when selecting international partners. Choose allies who demonstrate cultural sensitivity and adaptability to facilitate seamless collaboration across borders.

Legal and Regulatory Considerations: Ensure legal and regulatory compliance when forming strategic alliances. Seek legal counsel to negotiate partnership agreements and address potential legal implications of cross-border operations.

Commitment to Innovation and Growth: Partner with organisations committed to innovation and continuous growth. Foster a collaborative environment that encourages knowledge sharing, experimentation, and joint innovation initiatives.

Evaluate Track Record and Success Stories: Conduct due diligence on potential partners' track record and success stories in international markets. Learn from past experiences and case studies to inform your partnership decisions.

Choosing the right strategic alliances is a strategic imperative for successful global expansion. By prioritising shared values, complementary capabilities, and cultural compatibility, you can forge strong partnerships that propel your business forward in international markets. Invest in relationships that foster innovation, drive growth, and position your organisation for sustained success on a global scale.

It's evident that crisis management isn't just about weathering the storm, it's about harnessing its power to emerge stronger and more resilient than ever before. In the ever-evolving landscape of business, crises are not roadblocks; they're opportunities for growth, innovation, and transformation.

Throughout this chapter, we've explored the art of navigating high-pressure situations with finesse and fortitude. We've delved into the strategies and tactics needed to turn disasters into opportunities and to lead with unwavering resolve in the face of chaos. But more than that, we've uncovered the true essence of badassery in crisis management: the ability to rise above adversity, to adapt and pivot, and to emerge victorious against all odds.

As you reflect on the lessons learned in this chapter, remember that resilience isn't just about bouncing back, it's about bouncing back stronger, wiser, and more determined than ever before. It's about embracing the challenges, seizing the opportunities, and leading with courage and conviction in the darkest of times.

So, as you navigate the unpredictable waters of crisis management, do so with confidence, knowing that you have the skills, the mindset, and the badassery to conquer whatever challenges may come your way. Embrace the chaos, face it head-on, and emerge victorious on the other side. After all, in the world of badass business, there's no such thing as a crisis, only opportunities in disguise.

Task 10

Use this Crisis Response Plan Template to prepare your organisation for potential crises, mitigate risks, and demonstrate resilience and finesse in handling high-pressure situations effectively.

Crisis Response Plan Template: Develop a comprehensive crisis response plan with this template to handle high-pressure situations with finesse.

Crisis Response Plan Template

Instructions: Use this template to develop a comprehensive crisis response plan for handling high-pressure situations with finesse. Follow the sections below to outline key elements of your crisis response strategy and ensure readiness to address potential crises effectively.

1. **Crisis Identification:**
    - Define potential crisis scenarios that could impact your business or organisation.

2. **Response Team Formation:**
    - Identify key members of the crisis response team and their roles and responsibilities.

3. **Communication Strategy:**
    - Establish protocols for internal and external communication during a crisis, including key messages and channels.

4. **Risk Assessment and Impact Analysis:**
    - Conduct a risk assessment to evaluate potential consequences and impacts of each crisis scenario.

5. **Resource Allocation:**
    - Determine resource requirements (e.g., personnel, equipment, funding) needed to respond to crises effectively.

6. **Action Plan Development:**
    - Develop specific action plans for each identified crisis scenario, outlining steps and timelines for response.

7. **Training and Preparedness:**
    - Provide training and preparedness drills for the crisis response team to ensure readiness and effectiveness.

8. **Stakeholder Engagement:**

- Identify stakeholders (e.g., employees, customers, media) and define engagement strategies during a crisis.

9. **Continuous Monitoring and Evaluation:**
    - Establish mechanisms for continuous monitoring of crisis situations and evaluate response effectiveness.

10. **Post-Crisis Review and Learning:**
    - Conduct post-crisis reviews to identify lessons learned and update crisis response plans accordingly.

I hope this Crisis Response Plan Template proves valuable for developing a comprehensive crisis response strategy and ensuring readiness to handle high-pressure situations with finesse.

Chapter 11

Global Domination

Thinking small is simply not an option. It's time to set your sights on the global stage and unleash your ambitions on a worldwide scale. Just look at the example set by Richard Branson, the daring entrepreneur behind the Virgin Group. Branson's fearless approach to business has seen him expand his empire into countless industries, from music and airlines to space travel. By thinking big and refusing to be confined by borders or boundaries, Branson has cemented his legacy as a true global visionary.

So, strap in and prepare for the ride of a lifetime as we embark on a journey of international conquest and cultural intelligence. From forging strategic alliances to entering new markets with swagger, we'll equip you with the tools, tactics, and mindset needed to accelerate your path to world domination. Take a page from Branson's playbook and dare to dream on a global scale, because in the world of business, the sky's the limit for those with the courage to reach for the stars.

But make no mistake, global domination isn't for the faint of heart. It requires courage, vision, and a willingness to push the boundaries of what's possible. If you're ready to break free from the constraints of the status quo and unleash your full potential on a global scale, then this chapter is your ticket to greatness. So channel your inner Branson, embrace the spirit of adventure, and prepare to conquer new frontiers like never before. The world is waiting, and it's time to show them what you're made of.

Expanding Your Empire Internationally

In the pursuit of global domination, expanding your business empire internationally requires strategic planning, adaptability, and a bold vision. This chapter explores key considerations and actionable strategies for successfully expanding your business into international markets.

Market Research and Analysis: Conduct comprehensive market research to identify potential international markets that align with your business goals and target audience. Analyse market trends, consumer preferences, and competitive landscapes to inform your expansion strategy.

Develop a Market Entry Strategy: Define a clear market entry strategy tailored to each target market. Evaluate entry options such as exporting, licensing, joint ventures, or establishing subsidiaries, considering regulatory requirements and cultural nuances.

Cultural Intelligence and Adaptability: Cultivate cultural intelligence and adaptability to navigate diverse cultural landscapes. Understand local customs, values, and business etiquette to build rapport and foster positive relationships.

Legal and Regulatory Compliance: Ensure compliance with international laws, regulations, and trade policies. Seek legal counsel to navigate complex regulatory frameworks and mitigate legal risks associated with cross-border operations.

Build Strategic Partnerships: Form strategic partnerships with local stakeholders, distributors, or suppliers to facilitate market entry and expansion. Leverage existing networks and alliances to gain market insights and access resources.

Localisation of Products and Services: Adapt your products or services to suit local preferences and market demands. Customise marketing campaigns, packaging, and pricing strategies to resonate with international consumers.

Invest in Global Talent: Build a diverse and talented workforce capable of driving international growth. Recruit local talent with expertise in international markets and cultural insights to support business expansion.

Establish Strong Distribution Channels: Develop robust distribution channels to reach target customers efficiently. Explore partnerships with local distributors, e-commerce platforms, or retailers to expand market reach.

Invest in Brand Building and Marketing: Invest in brand building and marketing initiatives to raise awareness and establish credibility in new markets. Tailor marketing messages and promotional activities to resonate with diverse audiences.

Monitor and Adapt: Continuously monitor market dynamics and adapt your strategies accordingly. Stay agile and responsive to changing market conditions, consumer preferences, and competitive landscapes.

Expanding your empire internationally presents immense opportunities for growth and diversification. By adopting a strategic and culturally sensitive approach, you can navigate the complexities of international expansion and position your business for global success. Embrace the challenge of global domination with ambition, resilience, and a commitment to excellence.

Cultural Intelligence: Business Beyond Borders

In the thrilling pursuit of global domination, understanding the intricacies of different cultures isn't just a nice-to-have it's an absolute game-changer. Welcome to the world of cultural intelligence, where business transcends borders and success knows no bounds..

Gone are the days when business was confined to familiar territory. Today, to truly thrive in the global marketplace, you need to be fluent not just in market trends, but in the languages, customs, and traditions of diverse cultures. Cultivating cultural intelligence isn't just about being politically correct, it's about forging genuine connections, showing respect, and understanding the unique nuances that shape business interactions around the world.

Develop Cross-Cultural Awareness: Invest time in learning about different cultures, customs, and social norms in target markets. Understand the values, traditions, and communication styles that shape business interactions.

Adapt Communication Styles: Tailor your communication style to resonate with diverse cultural preferences. Use language and gestures that convey respect and openness and be mindful of non-verbal cues.

Build Trust and Rapport: Foster trust and rapport with international partners, clients, and stakeholders. Demonstrate empathy, humility, and genuine interest in understanding cultural perspectives.

Embrace Diversity and Inclusion: Embrace diversity within your organisation and value diverse perspectives. Create an inclusive culture that celebrates cultural differences and promotes collaboration across borders.

Navigate Cultural Etiquette: Familiarise yourself with cultural etiquette and protocol in international business settings. Be aware of proper greetings, gift-giving customs, and business etiquette to avoid cultural misunderstandings.

Adapt Products and Services: Modify products or services to align with local preferences and cultural sensitivities. Consider factors such as language, packaging, branding, and product features to appeal to international consumers.

Bridge Cultural Differences: Act as a bridge between cultures by facilitating cross-cultural understanding and collaboration. Encourage open dialogue and mutual respect to bridge cultural differences and build strong relationships.

Seek Local Expertise: Collaborate with local experts, consultants, or advisors who possess deep cultural insights and market knowledge. Leverage their expertise to navigate cultural nuances and make informed business decisions.

Demonstrate Cultural Sensitivity: Show sensitivity to cultural diversity in all business interactions. Avoid assumptions or stereotypes, and approach cross-cultural communication with curiosity and humility.

Continuous Learning and Adaptation: Embrace a mindset of continuous learning and adaptation. Stay curious, seek feedback, and reflect on experiences to enhance cultural intelligence and effectiveness in global business.

Cultural intelligence is a critical skill for expanding your business empire internationally. By embracing cultural diversity, demonstrating sensitivity, and fostering cross-cultural collaboration, you can build strong relationships, navigate challenges, and unlock new opportunities on the global stage. Embrace the richness of global cultures and leverage cultural intelligence as a strategic advantage in your international expansion journey.

Strategic Alliances: Choosing the Right Partners

Strategic alliances are the secret weapon in your arsenal. But not just any partnership will do, it's crucial to choose your allies with precision and foresight. This subsection is your guide to selecting the right partners for your international expansion efforts, ensuring that every alliance you forge is a stepping stone towards world domination.

Picture this: you're at the helm of your empire, charting a course towards uncharted territories. But to navigate the treacherous waters of international expansion, you need more than just a map you need a crew of trusted allies by your side. Strategic alliances provide the fuel for your journey, offering access to resources, expertise, and market insights that can propel your global growth strategy to new heights.

But here's the catch: not all partnerships are created equal. To truly succeed on the world stage, you need to choose your allies with care, precision, and a keen eye for mutual benefit. From industry titans to emerging disruptors, the right partners can mean the difference between triumph and defeat.

Here's how to choose the right partners for your international endeavours:

Align with Shared Goals and Values: Look for partners who share similar goals, values, and vision for business expansion. Ensure alignment in long-term objectives and commitment to mutual success.

Complementary Capabilities: Seek partners with complementary capabilities and strengths that enhance your competitive advantage in international markets. Identify areas of synergy where collaboration can drive innovation and market penetration.

Market Knowledge and Expertise: Prioritise partners with deep market knowledge and expertise in target regions. Choose allies who understand local regulations, consumer behaviours, and market dynamics to navigate complexities effectively.

Established Reputation and Credibility: Partner with reputable organisations or industry leaders known for their credibility and integrity. Leverage their brand reputation and network to build trust and credibility in new markets.

Compatibility and Trust: Build partnerships based on mutual trust, transparency, and compatibility. Establish clear communication channels and governance structures to foster collaboration and resolve potential conflicts.

Risk-sharing and Resource Allocation: Evaluate risk-sharing and resource allocation strategies with potential partners. Explore mutual investment opportunities and shared responsibilities to optimise operational efficiency and minimise risks.

Cultural Compatibility: Consider cultural compatibility and alignment when selecting international partners. Choose allies who demonstrate cultural sensitivity and adaptability to facilitate seamless collaboration across borders.

Legal and Regulatory Considerations: Ensure legal and regulatory compliance when forming strategic alliances. Seek legal counsel to negotiate partnership agreements and address potential legal implications of cross-border operations.

Commitment to Innovation and Growth: Partner with organisations committed to innovation and continuous growth. Foster a collaborative environment that encourages knowledge sharing, experimentation, and joint innovation initiatives.

Evaluate Track Record and Success Stories: Conduct due diligence on potential partners' track record and success stories in international markets. Learn from past experiences and case studies to inform your partnership decisions.

Choosing the right strategic alliances is a strategic imperative for successful global expansion. By prioritising shared values, complementary capabilities, and cultural compatibility, you can forge strong partnerships that propel your business forward in international markets. Invest in relationships that foster innovation, drive growth, and position your organisation for sustained success on a global scale.

it's clear that the journey to global domination is not for the faint of heart. It's a thrilling adventure filled with challenges, triumphs, and the exhilarating pursuit of greatness on a global scale. Throughout this chapter, we've explored the essential strategies, tactics, and mindset required to expand your empire beyond borders and claim your stake on the international stage.

From forging strategic alliances to mastering cultural intelligence, we've equipped you with the tools and insights needed to navigate the complexities of global business with confidence and finesse. But beyond the practicalities, we've also tapped into the essence of what it means to be a true global leader, a visionary who dares to dream big, break boundaries, and defy the status quo in pursuit of a bold and audacious vision.

So, as you embark on your journey towards global domination, remember this: the world is yours for the taking, but success will not come easy. It will require dedication, perseverance, and a relentless commitment to excellence in everything you do. But with the knowledge, skills you've acquired in this chapter, there's no limit to what you can achieve. So go forth, conquer new horizons, and leave your mark on the world. After all, in the world of badass business, the sky's the limit, and beyond.

Task 11

Use this Market Entry Strategy Framework to plan and execute your international expansion strategy effectively, maximise market opportunities, and achieve global domination in your industry.

Market Entry Strategy Framework: Plan your international expansion using this strategic framework for entering new markets.

Market Entry Strategy Framework

Instructions: Use this strategic framework to plan your international expansion and market entry strategy effectively. Follow the sections below to outline key elements of your market entry plan and ensure a successful global domination strategy.

1. **Market Analysis:**
   - Conduct comprehensive research to identify target markets and assess market potential, including market size, growth trends, and competitive landscape.

2. **Market Segmentation and Targeting:**
   - Segment target markets based on demographics, psychographics, and behavioural factors.
   - Prioritise specific market segments for initial market entry based on strategic fit and growth opportunities.

3. **Entry Mode Selection:**
   - Evaluate various market entry modes (e.g., exporting, licensing, joint ventures, wholly owned subsidiaries) based on market characteristics and organisational capabilities.
   - Select the most appropriate entry mode that aligns with your strategic objectives and risk tolerance.

4. **Legal and Regulatory Considerations:**
   - Identify legal and regulatory requirements for market entry in target countries, including intellectual property protection, trade regulations, and tax implications.
   - Ensure compliance with local laws and regulations to mitigate legal risks.

5. **Resource Allocation and Investment Strategy:**

- Determine resource requirements (e.g., financial, human capital, technological) for market entry and expansion.
- Develop an investment strategy that aligns with budget constraints and expected returns on investment.

6. **Market Entry Timeline and Milestones:**
   - Establish a timeline with key milestones for market entry and expansion activities.
   - Set realistic deadlines and milestones to track progress and ensure timely execution of market entry strategy.

7. **Distribution and Channel Strategy:**
   - Develop a distribution and channel strategy to reach target customers efficiently and effectively.
   - Identify potential distribution partners, agents, or distributors to facilitate market penetration.

8. **Marketing and Branding Strategy:**
   - Develop a tailored marketing and branding strategy for each target market.
   - Adapt marketing messages, channels, and tactics to resonate with local preferences and cultural nuances.

9. **Risk Assessment and Contingency Planning:**
   - Identify potential risks associated with market entry (e.g., currency fluctuations, political instability) and develop contingency plans.

- Implement risk mitigation strategies to minimise potential disruptions to market entry activities.

10. **Monitoring and Evaluation:**
    - Establish metrics and KPIs to monitor the performance of market entry activities.
    - Conduct regular evaluations to assess the effectiveness of the market entry strategy and make adjustments as needed.

Chapter 12

Future-Proofing
Your Business

Staying ahead of the curve isn't just a strategic advantage, it's a survival imperative. Welcome to Chapter 12, where we dive deep into the art of future-proofing your business against the winds of change and uncertainty. In this chapter, we'll explore the strategies, tactics, and mindset needed to anticipate the unexpected, adapt to emerging trends, and ensure that your empire stands the test of time.

As we embark on this journey of future-proofing, it's worth drawing inspiration from notable business leaders who have mastered the art of resilience and foresight. Take, for example, Jeff Bezos, the visionary founder of Amazon. Bezos didn't just build a company he built a relentless innovation machine that thrives on disruption and change. By constantly scanning the horizon for emerging trends and embracing a culture of experimentation and adaptation, Bezos transformed Amazon from a humble online bookstore into a global behemoth that reshaped the retail landscape forever.

Similarly, Elon Musk, the enigmatic CEO of Tesla and SpaceX, has demonstrated a remarkable ability to future-proof his businesses against the forces of obsolescence. From electric cars to space exploration, Musk has consistently pushed the boundaries of what's possible, leveraging technological innovation and visionary leadership to stay one step ahead of the competition. His unwavering commitment to sustainability, coupled with his relentless pursuit of audacious goals, serves as a testament to the power of future-proofing in the face of uncertainty.

So, as we delve into the strategies and tactics of future-proofing your business, let's draw inspiration from the trailblazers who have come before us. Let's embrace the spirit of innovation, resilience, and adaptability that defines the most successful entrepreneurs of our time.

Anticipating the Unanticipated

The ability to anticipate and adapt to unforeseen challenges is more than a skill, it's a necessity for survival and success. "Anticipating the Unanticipated" isn't just about being reactive; it's about being proactively prepared for the future, whatever it may bring. This chapter will guide you through the process of future-proofing your business, emphasising the need for foresight, innovation, and a robust readiness strategy that can handle the unexpected.

The cornerstone of anticipating the unanticipated lies in developing a forward-thinking mindset that continuously scans the horizon for potential disruptions. This involves staying informed about emerging trends and technologies, understanding the evolving needs of your customers, and being aware of the broader economic and social changes that could impact your industry. By fostering a culture of learning and curiosity within your organisation, you encourage a proactive approach to business strategy.

Innovation plays a critical role in this process. It's not just about creating new products or services; it's about constantly refining your business model to adapt to new market conditions and opportunities. For instance, consider how Netflix transitioned from a DVD rental service to a streaming giant. They didn't just adapt to changes in technology, they anticipated the shift in consumer behaviour towards on-demand entertainment, positioning themselves ahead of the curve and redefining the industry in the process.

Moreover, future-proofing your business means building flexibility into your operations and financial planning. This can involve diversifying your revenue streams, investing in scalable technologies, and developing contingency plans that allow you to pivot quickly in response to unforeseen events. By establishing a strong foundation of adaptability, you ensure that your business can not only withstand future shocks but also seize new opportunities that arise from unexpected changes.

Here we will provide you with practical advice and actionable insights to safeguard and propel your business into the future.

Embrace a Culture of Innovation: Foster a culture that encourages experimentation, creativity, and forward thinking. Empower your team to challenge norms, explore new ideas, and adapt swiftly to emerging trends.

Continuous Environmental Scanning: Stay vigilant and proactive in monitoring market trends, technological advancements, and regulatory changes. Anticipate shifts in consumer preferences and industry dynamics to identify potential opportunities and threats.

Scenario Planning and Risk Assessment: Conduct scenario planning exercises to simulate future scenarios and assess their impact on your business. Identify key risks and develop contingency plans to mitigate potential disruptions.

Invest in Emerging Technologies: Embrace emerging technologies that have the potential to disrupt your industry. Leverage innovation to enhance operational efficiency, improve customer experiences, and drive competitive advantage.

Adaptability and Flexibility: Cultivate adaptability and flexibility within your organisation. Build agile processes and organisational structures that can pivot quickly in response to changing circumstances.

Collaborate with Industry Leaders: Form strategic partnerships with industry leaders, startups, and research institutions to leverage collective expertise and stay abreast of industry developments.

Customer-Centric Innovation: Prioritise customer needs and preferences when developing new products or services. Leverage customer feedback and data analytics to drive customer-centric innovation and enhance brand loyalty.

Invest in Talent Development: Build a skilled and adaptable workforce capable of navigating future challenges. Invest in continuous learning and development to equip employees with the skills needed for tomorrow's opportunities.

Sustainability and Social Responsibility: Integrate sustainability and social responsibility into your business strategy. Embrace environmentally friendly practices and demonstrate a commitment to ethical business practices.

Strategic Diversification: Diversify your revenue streams and market presence to reduce dependence on specific markets or products. Explore new growth opportunities and expand into adjacent industries or geographies.

Future-proofing your business is a proactive endeavour that requires foresight, agility, and a willingness to embrace change. By adopting a strategic approach to innovation, risk management, and talent development, you can position your business to thrive in an uncertain future. Anticipate the unanticipated and lead your organisation towards sustained success and resilience in the face of evolving challenges.

Sustainability and Business Continuity Planning

In the ever-changing dynamics of the modern business world, sustainability has transcended its initial environmental connotations to become a crucial element of strategic business planning. "Sustainability and Business Continuity Planning" is not just about preserving resources; it's about creating a resilient, adaptable business model that thrives on long-term visions and responsible governance. This section will delve into how embedding sustainability into your business continuity strategies can lead to enhanced operational efficiency, risk mitigation, and, ultimately, sustainable growth.

At its core, integrating sustainability into business continuity planning involves aligning environmental, social, and corporate governance (ESG) goals with business objectives to create a synergy that not only protects but also enriches your business environment. This approach helps companies navigate regulatory landscapes, meet stakeholder expectations, and appeal to a growing base of consumers who prioritise corporate responsibility in their purchasing decisions.

Operational efficiency is significantly enhanced through sustainable practices. For example, reducing waste or optimising energy use not only cuts costs but also minimises environmental impact, creating a leaner, more agile operation. Companies like Patagonia, which has built sustainability into every aspect of its operations, from supply chain management to product design, demonstrate how these practices can reduce costs, drive innovation, and create a competitive advantage in the market.

Risk mitigation is another critical aspect of integrating sustainability into continuity planning. Environmental risks, such as climate change-induced disruptions, or social risks, like shifts in consumer behaviour towards ethical consumption, can pose significant threats to business as usual. By anticipating and planning for these risks, businesses can not only avoid potential pitfalls but also position themselves as leaders in a future where sustainability becomes the norm, not the exception. So, how and what do you need to do? Well that's simple:

Align Sustainability Goals with Business Objectives: Integrate sustainability goals into your overall business strategy. Align environmental, social, and governance (ESG) initiatives with core business objectives to create synergies and drive value.

Identify Environmental Risks and Opportunities: Conduct a thorough assessment of environmental risks and opportunities that impact your business. Identify potential vulnerabilities such as resource scarcity, regulatory changes, and climate-related risks.

Implement Sustainable Practices: Adopt sustainable business practices across your value chain. Reduce carbon emissions, minimise waste generation, and optimise resource use to enhance operational efficiency and reduce environmental impact.

Build Resilience Through Diversity: Embrace diversity and inclusion within your organisation. Foster a diverse workforce and supplier base to enhance resilience and adaptability in the face of market disruptions.

Strengthen Supply Chain Resilience: Assess supply chain vulnerabilities and incorporate sustainability criteria into supplier selection and relationship management. Build resilient supply chains that prioritise ethical sourcing and transparency.

Develop Contingency Plans for Environmental Risks: Create contingency plans for potential environmental risks and disruptions. Implement measures to mitigate the impact of natural disasters, climate change, and other environmental challenges.

Engage Stakeholders and Communities: Collaborate with stakeholders, local communities, and NGOs to address sustainability challenges collaboratively. Build partnerships that foster positive social impact and contribute to community resilience.

Invest in Renewable Energy and Technology: Embrace renewable energy solutions and innovative technologies to reduce dependence on fossil fuels and minimise environmental footprint. Explore opportunities for sustainable innovation and green technology adoption.

Measure and Monitor Progress: Establish key performance indicators (KPIs) and metrics to track sustainability performance. Regularly assess progress towards sustainability goals and adjust strategies as needed to drive continuous improvement.

Communicate Transparently: Communicate your sustainability efforts transparently to stakeholders, investors, and customers. Demonstrate commitment to sustainable practices and corporate responsibility to build trust and credibility.

By integrating sustainability into your business continuity planning, you can strengthen operational resilience, mitigate environmental risks, and position your business for long-term success in a changing world. Embrace sustainability as a catalyst for innovation and growth and leverage its transformative potential to future-proof your business against emerging challenges and opportunities.

Legacy Building: Ensuring Your Empire Lasts

As you future-proof your business through sustainability and strategic planning, it's essential to consider the legacy you wish to leave behind. Legacy building is about creating a lasting impact and ensuring the longevity of your empire beyond your tenure. Here are key principles for building a sustainable legacy:

Define Your Vision and Values: Clarify your vision and values as a foundation for legacy building. Articulate a purpose-driven mission that transcends short-term goals and aligns with enduring principles.

Cultivate Ethical Leadership: Lead with integrity and ethical principles. Demonstrate a commitment to responsible business practices, transparency, and accountability in all aspects of your operations.

Invest in Succession Planning: Develop a robust succession plan to ensure continuity of leadership and governance. Identify and groom future leaders within your organisation who embody your values and vision.

Promote a Culture of Learning and Innovation: Foster a culture of continuous learning, adaptation, and innovation. Encourage experimentation and risk-taking to drive evolution and relevance in a rapidly changing world.

Engage Stakeholders in Long-Term Planning: Collaborate with stakeholders—including employees, customers, suppliers, and communities—to co-create sustainable solutions and initiatives. Build enduring relationships based on shared values and mutual benefit.

Prioritise Environmental and Social Impact: Integrate environmental and social impact considerations into your business strategy. Implement sustainable practices that contribute positively to society and minimise negative externalities.

Support Community Development: Invest in community development initiatives and philanthropic efforts. Make meaningful contributions to social causes and support local communities to create a positive legacy of impact.

Document and Share Your Story: Document your journey and achievements as a testament to your legacy. Share your experiences, insights, and lessons learned to inspire future generations and contribute to collective knowledge.

Commit to Continuous Improvement: Embrace a mindset of continuous improvement and evolution. Adapt to changing circumstances, embrace emerging trends, and evolve your legacy strategy over time.

Measure Impact and Celebrate Milestones: Establish metrics to measure the impact of your legacy-building efforts. Celebrate milestones and achievements with stakeholders to reinforce commitment and inspire ongoing dedication.

Building a lasting legacy requires foresight, dedication, and a commitment to leaving a positive imprint on the world. By integrating sustainability, ethical leadership, and long-term planning into your business strategy, you can ensure that your empire endures and continues to thrive for generations to come.

As we bring this book to a close, it's clear that future-proofing your business is not just a strategic imperative it's a mindset, a philosophy, and a commitment to excellence that transcends the present moment. Throughout this chapter, we've explored the strategies, tactics, and mindset needed to anticipate the unexpected, adapt to emerging trends, and ensure that your empire stands the test of time.

But future-proofing isn't just about building a fortress against uncertainty it's about embracing change, seizing opportunities, and shaping the future on your own terms. It's about daring to dream big, challenging the status quo, and pushing the boundaries of what's possible. And above all, it's about building a legacy that transcends generations one that leaves an indelible mark on the world long after you're gone.

So as you reflect on the insights and lessons shared in this chapter, remember this: the future belongs to those who are bold enough to create it. By cultivating a mindset of resilience, innovation, and adaptability, you can navigate the winds of change with confidence and chart a course towards a brighter tomorrow.

As you embark on the journey of future-proofing your business, may you be guided by the wisdom of the past, inspired by the possibilities of the future, and driven by a relentless commitment to excellence. And may your empire stand as a beacon of success, resilience, and visionary leadership in a world that is constantly evolving. After all, in the game of business, the only certainty is uncertainty and those who are prepared to embrace it will emerge stronger, wiser, and more triumphant than ever before.

Final Task

Use this Future Trends Radar to proactively monitor, assess, and respond to future trends and disruptions in your industry. By staying ahead of the curve, you can future-proof your business and seize opportunities for growth and innovation.

Future Trends Radar: Stay ahead of the curve by monitoring future trends and disruptions with this radar tool.

Future Trends Radar

Instructions: Use this radar tool to stay ahead of the curve by monitoring future trends and disruptions in your industry. Regularly assess and update your radar to anticipate changes and future-proof your business effectively.

Identify Key Trends:

- List current and emerging trends that could impact your industry or market landscape (e.g., technological advancements, regulatory changes, consumer preferences).

1. **Assess Impact and Importance:**

    - Evaluate the potential impact and importance of each trend on your business operations and strategy.
    - Rate trends based on relevance, urgency, and potential consequences (1 = Low Impact/Importance, 5 = High Impact/Importance).

2. **Monitor and Track Trends:**
   - Continuously monitor industry publications, market reports, and expert insights to track the progression of identified trends.
   - Stay informed about new developments and emerging signals related to each trend.

3. **Scenario Planning:**
   - Develop scenarios and hypotheses based on identified trends to anticipate potential futures.
   - Consider best-case, worst-case, and moderate scenarios to inform strategic decision-making.

4. **Adaptation and Innovation:**
   - Identify opportunities for innovation and adaptation based on anticipated trends.
   - Explore ways to leverage trends to enhance competitiveness and future-proof your business.

5. **Cross-Functional Collaboration:**
   - Foster cross-functional collaboration within your organisation to leverage diverse perspectives and insights related to future trends.
   - Engage key stakeholders in trend analysis and scenario planning activities.

Example:

1. **Identify Key Trends:**

    - Trend 1: Artificial Intelligence and Automation in Manufacturing.

    - Trend 2: Shift towards Sustainable and Eco-friendly Practices.

    - Trend 3: Rise of E-commerce and Digital Transformation.

2. **Assess Impact and Importance:**

    - Trend 1: High Impact/Importance (5)

    - Trend 2: Moderate Impact/Importance (3)

    - Trend 3: High Impact/Importance (4)

3. **Monitor and Track Trends:**

    - Subscribe to industry newsletters, attend conferences, and follow thought leaders on social media to stay updated on trends.

4. **Scenario Planning:**

    - Scenario 1: Rapid adoption of AI leads to increased productivity but requires workforce reskilling.

    - Scenario 2: Growing demand for sustainable products drives market differentiation and brand loyalty.

5. **Adaptation and Innovation:**

- Invest in AI technologies to streamline production processes and enhance operational efficiency.
- Introduce eco-friendly product lines and sustainable packaging options to meet consumer demand.

6. **Cross-Functional Collaboration:**
    - Convene cross-functional workshops or brainstorming sessions to discuss trend implications and strategic responses.

Afterword

Keep Being Badass: A Lifelong Commitment

Congratulations on reaching the end of this journey towards becoming a true badass in the world of business. Remember, being badass isn't just a title, it's a mindset, a commitment, and a way of life. As you reflect on the insights and strategies shared in this book, I encourage you to embrace the following principles as you continue your entrepreneurial journey:

Embrace Change and Innovation: Stay agile and adaptable in the face of change. Embrace innovation as a driver of growth and transformation within your business.

Lead with Purpose and Integrity: Let your actions be guided by a clear sense of purpose and integrity. Lead with honesty, transparency, and a commitment to ethical business practices.

Invest in Continuous Learning: Commit to lifelong learning and personal development. Stay curious, seek new knowledge, and cultivate diverse perspectives to fuel innovation and growth.

Build Strong Relationships: Value relationships as the cornerstone of success. Cultivate meaningful connections with stakeholders, employees, customers, and partners based on trust, respect, and mutual benefit.

Stay Resilient and Persistent: Expect challenges along the way and embrace them as opportunities for growth. Stay resilient, persistent, and determined in pursuing your goals.

Give Back and Pay It Forward: Use your success as a platform to give back to your community and support causes that matter to you. Make a positive impact and inspire others to follow in your footsteps.

Celebrate Achievements and Milestones: Take time to acknowledge and celebrate your achievements and milestones.

Reflect on how far you've come and use these moments of success to fuel your passion and drive.

Remember, being a badass business leader isn't about being perfect it's about being bold, innovative, and unapologetically yourself. Keep pushing boundaries, challenging norms, and striving for greatness. Your journey towards global domination and business success is just beginning keep being badass every step of the way!

All of the tools, templates, and resources throughout this book are designed to empower you on your journey towards badass business success. Use them to implement the concepts discussed in each chapter and drive meaningful change within your organisation. Remember, the path to greatness is paved with determination, innovation, and a commitment to continuous improvement. Keep being a badass and turning your business dreams into reality!

Embrace the Journey

In the pursuit of success, it's easy to get caught up in the destination, the goals, and the end results. But true fulfilment comes from embracing the journey itself. Every step you take, every challenge you face, and every setback you encounter is a crucial part of your story. It's in these moments of struggle and perseverance that you build resilience, gain wisdom, and grow stronger.

Remember that success isn't a straight line; it's a winding path filled with twists and turns. Embrace each twist as an opportunity to learn and adapt. View setbacks not as failures, but as lessons that guide you towards a better, more refined version of yourself and your vision. The most impactful leaders and innovators are those who have faced adversity head-on and emerged stronger, with stories that inspire others.

Passion and purpose are the driving forces behind any significant achievement. When you align your efforts with what truly matters to you, the journey becomes not only bearable but exhilarating. Wake up each day with a clear sense of purpose, and let that fuel your actions. Pursue your goals with relentless determination, but also take the time to appreciate the progress you're making along the way.

Surround yourself with people who challenge and uplift you. Build a network of mentors, peers, and supporters who believe in your vision and push you to be your best self. Collaboration and shared experiences enrich your journey, providing you with new perspectives and valuable insights. Together, you can overcome obstacles that might seem insurmountable on your own.

Most importantly, be kind to yourself. Recognise that growth takes time, and be patient with your progress. Celebrate your victories, no matter how small, and use them as motivation to keep moving forward. Acknowledge your efforts and give yourself credit for the hard work you're putting in.

In the end, success is not just about reaching the top; it's about the person you become along the way. Embrace the journey with an open heart and a determined spirit. Stay true to your vision, remain resilient in the face of challenges, and let each step forward be a testament to your unwavering commitment to your dreams.

Thank you for joining me on this adventure. Here's to your continued success, growth, and impact in the world of business. Stay fearless, stay focused, and keep being badass.

Signed, Joshua Leach-Aslam (JLA)

www.ingramcontent.com/pod-product-compliance
Lightning Source LLC
Chambersburg PA
CBHW071159240526
45470CB00017B/384